Practical English for Airlines and Tourism

항공관광실무영어

Karina Aei-Kyung Kim, Jenny In-Ju Park

Practical English for Airlines and Tourism

항공관광실무영어

Karina Aei-Kyung Kim, Jenny In-Ju Park

Illustrations by Kyung Joo Alexis Jang
Proofreading by Hanna Ough

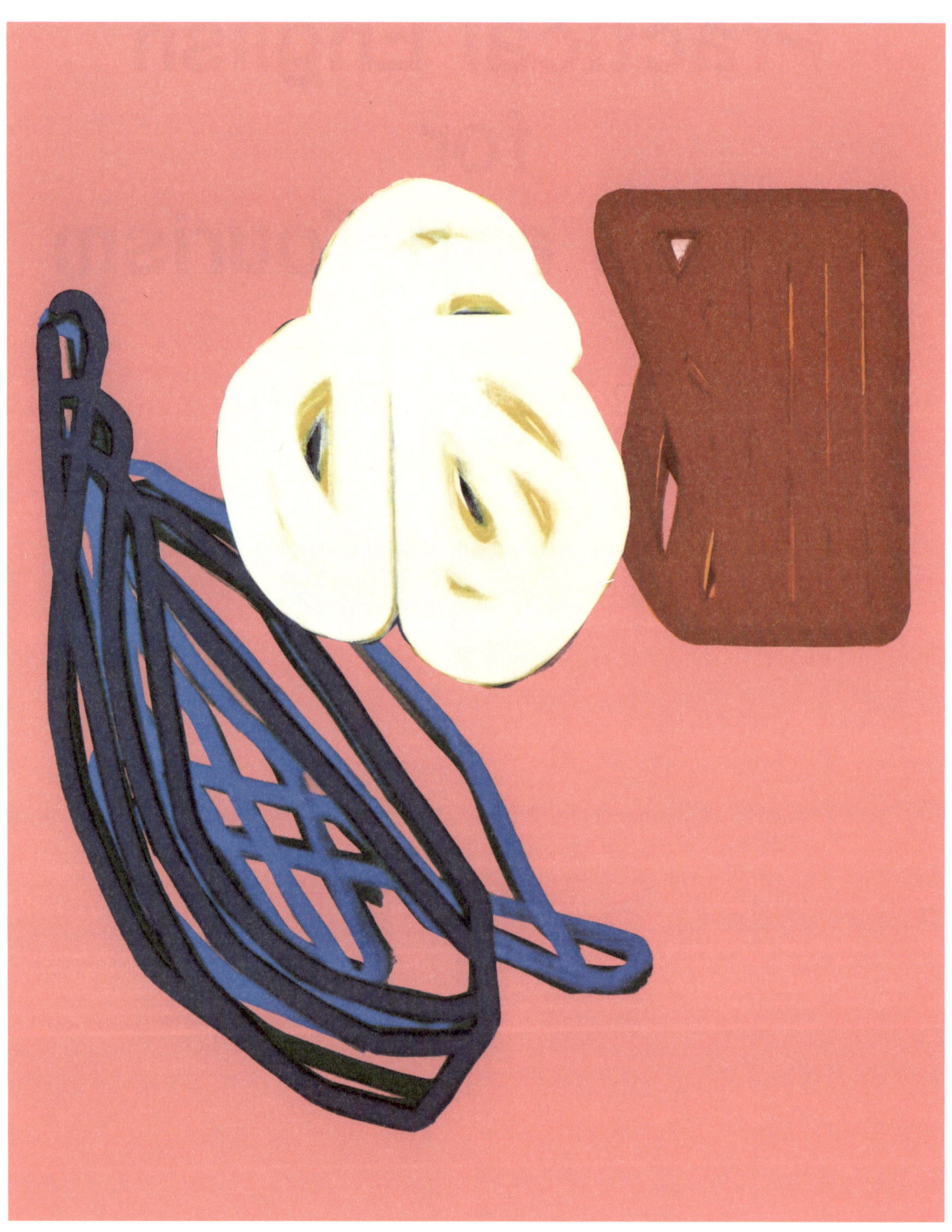

by SOO KYOUNG LEE

Preface

33년이란 오랜 비행 생활을 끝내고 학생들을 가르치면서, 승무원으로 생활하는 데에 기본적으로 필요한 영어회화의 폭은 기내 서비스를 중점으로 다루는 Cabin Service English 이외에도 아주 광범위하다는 것을 인식하고 있다. 본 교재는 비행 중 승객과의 접촉에서 사용하는 대화뿐만 아니라, 근무 중 공항이나 해외에서 또는 일상생활에서 사용할 수 있는 영어회화를 다양한 상황에 맞게 실용적으로 활용할 수 있도록 집필하였다. 또한 교재 속에서 다루어지는 내용은 향후 항공사 및 일반회사 입사 전형을 위한 준비단계를 염두에 두고 영어면접 시 다루어질 수 있는 내용을 포함하였다. 따라서 기내에서 쓰는 대화 및 가족, 취미, 학교, 날씨, 호텔, 레스토랑, 관광, 쇼핑, 직업 등 다양한 주제를 총 86편의 대화문에 포괄하여, 관광업 종사자는 물론 여행자나 일반인들도 언제든 숙지하고 영어로 대화하는 데 도움이 될 것으로 기대된다.

특히 본 교재는 학습자 혼자서 스스로 공부할 수 있도록 모든 대화문의 내용을 이해하기 쉽게 충분한 설명을 곁들였으며, 외국어를 공부하는데 필수적인 Listening, Reading, Speaking, and Writing Skills 이 네 가지를 다 향상시킬 수 있는 교과내용을 다루어 반복적으로 연습할 수 있도록 신경을 기울였다. 교재의 활용성을 최대화하기 위해 제작된 MP3를 통해 회화의 발음, 억양, 속도 등을 파악하면서 학습하기를 권장한다. 항공 및 관광업은 국제적 감각이 필요한 직업임을 고려하여 다른 나라의 문화와 관습을 이해하는 데 도움이 될 수 있는 흥미있는 내용으로 구성하고자 노력하였다. 이 기회를 통해 다른 국가, 인종, 언어 및 문화 등에 대한 관심이 높아지고, 그들을 바라보는 관점과 이해의 폭 또한 넓어져 진정한 글로벌 인재로 성장하기를 희망한다.

Contents

Part 1. Practical English for Airlines and Tourism

Unit 01　Greetings ··· 11
Unit 02　Family ··· 19
Unit 03　Hobby ·· 27
Unit 04　School ··· 35
Unit 05　Travel ·· 45
Unit 06　Airport ··· 55
Unit 07　Airplane ··· 63
Unit 08　Hotel ·· 73
Unit 09　Restaurant ·· 83
Unit 10　Weather ·· 91
Unit 11　Directions ··· 99
Unit 12　Appointment ··· 107
Unit 13　Shopping ·· 115
Unit 14　Food ·· 125
Unit 15　Job ·· 133

Part 2. Passenger Address Announcement

Korean Air ··· 144
Cathay Pacific Airways ·· 150

Part 3. Appendix

Useful Phrasal Verbs ··· 158
Irregular Verbs ··· 164

Answer Key ·· 167

PART 1

Practical English for Airlines and Tourism

unit 01	Greetings	11
unit 02	Family	19
unit 03	Hobby	27
unit 04	School	35
unit 05	Travel	45
unit 06	Airport	55
unit 07	Airplane	63
unit 08	Hotel	73
unit 09	Restaurant	83
unit 10	Weather	91
unit 11	Directions	99
unit 12	Appointment	107
unit 13	Shopping	115
unit 14	Food	125
unit 15	Job	133

Unit 01 Greetings

"How do you do? It's nice to meet you."

"Let us always meet each other with smile, for the smile is the beginning of love."
- Mother Teresa -

Dialogue 1

A : Hello. I'm Jane.
B : Hi, Jane. I'm Tom. (hold out his hand to shake)
A : Nice to meet you, Tom. Where are you from?
B : I'm from Canada. Our family lives in a small town near Toronto.
A : Canada. Wow! I've always wanted to go there. How long have you been in Korea?
B : I just arrived last week, and it's my first day of school.
A : Really? I think you'll love Seoul. It's a fun and interesting city. Many foreign students are studying in Korea.
B : I hope I can get along well with Korean students.
A : Don't worry. Koreans are quite open to foreigners. I'm sure you'll make many new friends here.
B : I hope so.

get along : 사이좋게 지내다, 의좋게 살다
Don't worry : 걱정하지마
be sure : .... 을 확신하다
make friends : 친구들을 사귀다

Dialogue 2

A : Hello, Tom. How are you?
B : Hi, Jane. Haven't seen you for a while. How are you doing?
A : Fine. And you?
B : I'm pretty good, thanks. I don't think you two know each other, do you? This is my friend James. May I introduce James Lee?
A : No, we've never met. How do you do, James? (hold out her hand to shake)
C : How do you do, Jane?
A : It's a pleasure to meet you.
C : The pleasure is mine.

소개를 받을 때 : 보통 "How do you do?" 또는 "Hello, Hi" 등으로 대답하며 악수를 한다. "How do you do?"는 질문이 아니며 상대도 "How do you do?"로 대답한다.

Dialogue 3

A : Good morning! Did you have a nice stay, sir?
B : Very well, thank you. The hotel was superb, and the service was excellent.
A : When are you leaving, sir?
B : The flight departure time is 11:00 a.m.
A : I see. Have you confirmed your ticket?
B : Yes, I did it a week ago.
A : Good. I hope you can come to Jeju again.
B : I hope so too. Thank you for your kindness. I had a great time here.
A : My pleasure. We look forward to having you stay here again in the near future. Have a pleasant journey back home.

flight departure time : 항공편 출발시간
confirm : 확인하다
look forward to + 명사 / -ing형 : …… 하기를 고대하다
My pleasure : 도움이 되어 저도 기뻐요 (고맙다는 말에 대한 정중한 인사)

Dialogue 4

A : Hi, Tom. Are you okay? You look sick.
B : I'm not very well. I caught the flu and have been coughing for a few days.
A : Did you see the doctor?
B : Yes, I did, two days ago.
A : What did the doctor say?
B : I need to take some medicines and rest in bed for two or three days.
A : That's too bad. Did you go to school then?
B : Yes, I went to school today because I didn't want to miss my class.
A : You are a good student. Take good care of yourself. I hope you get well soon.
B : I will. Keep in touch.

catch the flu : 독감에 걸리다 (= come down with the flu)
cough : 기침하다
miss : (수업에) 결석하다, 빠뜨리다
keep in touch : (또) 연락해요

Dialogue 5

A : Hello, James. Long time, no see. How everything is going with you?
B : So far so good. How about you?
A : Not too bad, thanks. How is your family?
B : They are all fine. How about yours? Please say hello to your family for me.
A : Sure, I will. By the way, we are having a barbecue party next weekend. If you are free, would you like to join us?
B : Are you? Of course, I'd love to join you guys.
A : I have also invited several friends from our high school days. I think, you may already know some of them.
B : Sounds great! It'll be good to catch up with them. What time are you going to start?
A : We will start around 5 p.m. You can come a little early, have a drink, and chat with our friends before dinner.
B : All right, I'll do that. Thanks for inviting me.

for a while : 잠시, 얼마동안 (for는 종종 생략 됨)
Please say hello to your family for me : 나를 대신해 가족들에게 안부 전해줘
By the way : 말이 나온 김에, 그런데
Of course : 물론, 당연히
join : (기다리고 있는 사람과) 만나다, 합류하다
guys : (남녀 상관없이, 무리지어 있는) 사람들
invite : 초대하다, 초청하다
high school days : 고등학교 시절
Sounds great! : 좋겠네요, 좋은 생각이예요
catch up : (오랫만에 만난 사람과 소식/안부 등을) 얘기하다
a little early : (어떤 정해진 시간보다) 조금 일찍
have a drink : 한잔하다
chat : 담소(잡담)하다, 수다 떨다
all right (= alright) : 그래, 좋아, 알았어

Useful Words and Expressions

1) Sentence Examples

How are you?	– Good! And you?
Hey! How are you doing?	– I'm doing well. How about yourself?
How have you been?	– Pretty good. Thanks.
How have you been doing?	– Great. / I'm tired.
Long time, no see. How is it going?	– Fine. How are you?
How's everything?	– (It) couldn't be better.
How everything is going?	– So far, so good.
How are things with you?	– Not (too) bad.
How are you getting along?	– Terrible.
Are you having a hard time?	– Well, it could be worse.
Hi, long time no see! What have you been up to?	– I went back to school in March, so I've just been taking classes.
What's up? (informal, casual greeting)	– Not much. How about you?

2) Make sentences out of the words below.

1. How / you / are / getting along?

   _____

2. Oh, / you / I / haven't seen / for ages.

   _____

3. It / to meet / my pleasure / was / you.

   _____

4. Tom, / I / may / introduce / my friend, Oliver Thorn?

   _____

3) Introduction

May I introduce Christopher Thorn? This is my colleague.
Can I introduce my friend, Fiona Simpson?
James, do you know Tom? Tom, this is my friend, James.
Sarah, I don't think you've met Jane. This is a friend of mine.
Have you met my mother? This is my mother.
I guess, you don't know my boyfriend, Andrew. This is Andrew.

4) Farewell

It has been nice talking to you.
It was nice to meet you. / It was nice meeting you.
It was a pleasure to see you. / It was my pleasure to meet you.
See you (again). / See you later. / See you tomorrow. / See you next week.
Have a nice / good / wonderful day. Take care.

5) Special Greetings

Merry Christmas! Happy New Year! Happy Easter!
Happy birthday! Happy wedding anniversary!
Congratulations on your new job / exam results / engagement!

Reading Comprehension - Korea

Language and culture are closely related and affect each other. Every language reflects what you think is important in that culture. The Korean language is one of the biggest advantages of the Korean culture because it is easy to read and write. In addition to it being easy to learn, Korean is the only language in the world with a correctly known date of creation as well as its founder. As a result, Korea's illiteracy rate is the lowest in the world. Recently, a Korean boy group called BTS appeared as speakers for UNICEF's event in New York, as they have shown a good influence on young people all around the world. The Korean government presented the group with a medal of culture in recognition of their effort of spreading, and promoting the Korean language and the Korean wave. Unlike other idol groups, the BTS boys have been singing about their "thoughts." They expressed their anxiety and hope, and included social issues in the lyrics of their songs at the same time. The BTS boy group is exceeding the value of being the successful Korean idol group in the global market because they try to convey their true feelings through their music on the stage.

illiteracy rate : 문맹률
anxiety and hope : 근심, 걱정과 희망
social issue : 사회적 문제
lyrics : (노래) 가사들

Conversation Practice

Please write your answers and practice with your partner.

Q1. How are you? / How are you doing?

Q2. May I have your name, please? / What's your name?

Q3. How old are you?

Q4. Where do you live?

Q5. What is your phone number?
What is your email address?

Q6. Where were you born?
Where is your hometown?
Can you tell me about your hometown?

Q7. What do you do? / What do you do for a living?

Unit 02 Family

"Can you tell me about your family?"

"Someone is sitting in the shade today because someone planted a tree a long time ago."
- Warren Buffett -

Dialogue 1

A : Can you tell me about your family?
B : There are four people in my family, my father, mother, sister, and me.
A : Is your sister older or younger than you?
B : She is my elder sister. What about you? How many people are there in your family?
A : I have my parents and two younger brothers. And we are living with our grandparents. All together we are seven.
B : Wow! That's a big family. Isn't your house a bit crowded?
A : Sometimes, but I like having a big family because there's always someone to talk to.
B : I guess that's true. Bigger families can be a lot of fun.

older-oldest vs. **elder-eldest**
- 가족 간의 순서를 언급할 때에는 older-oldest 대신에 **elder-eldest**를 쓸 수 있다.
  단, 명사를 수식하는 한정적 용법으로만 쓰이고, 서술적 용법으로는 쓰지 않는다.
- Her **eldest** / oldest son is a medical student.
crowded : 붐비는, 혼잡한

Dialogue 2

A : What does your father do, Tom?
B : My father is a policeman and currently working at the western district police station in Toronto as a senior police officer. He is very hard working, but satisfied with his job.
A : What is he like?
B : He is kind and generous. He really cares about people. I spend much time talking with my dad at home. I think he is a good father to me.
A : He seems to be very nice. I can see that you like him a lot.
B : Yes. I think so. I respect my dad the most, and he always encourages me to learn and experience the best things. That's why I'm here.

district : 지역, 구역
that's why : 그래서 ... 한다, 그런 까닭이야

Dialogue 3

A : How old are your parents?
B : They are in their mid-fifties. My father is fifty-six, and my mother is fifty-four years old.
A : Is your brother working?
B : No, my brother is in the army, and my sister is in high school. What about you?
A : I'm the only child of my parents. I don't have any sibling.
B : Do you live with your parents?
A : No, I'm living in the dormitory because my school is far from my home.
B : How often do you go home then?
A : I go home once a month.
B : Don't you miss your family?
A : Not really. I talk to them almost everyday.

in one's mid-fifties : 50대 중반의
be in the army : 군대에 있다
sibling : 형제, 자매
miss : 보고싶어하다, 그리워하다

Dialogue 4

A : What's your family like?
B : Well, my family consists of four members including: my father, mother, elder sister, and myself.
A : How old is your sister?
B : My sister is twenty-four, four years older than me. And she is working as a nurse at a hospital in Suwon. What about your family?
A : I have my parents and an older brother. My elder brother is working for Samsung Electronics and living in Seoul.
B : It's a good company. How long has he worked for the company?
A : He has been working there for five years.

consists of (something) : ..... 로 구성되다

Dialogue 5

A : Hi, Jane. I was wondering, are you free this Saturday?
B : Oh.... I have a family gathering in the evening. Why? What did you have in mind?
A : I was thinking of going to the cinema with you. There's a good movie showing now, but if you're not available......
B : Well, it sounds like fun, but unfortunately, I'll be very busy on Saturday.
A : What do you have to do?
B : I have to pick up my grandparents at the airport in the morning, then help my parents prepare for the gathering in the afternoon.
A : Huh.... You will be very busy.
B : But thanks a lot for asking me. Maybe next time.
A : That's fine. We'll make it next time.
B : If you don't mind, I'd be delighted to have you over and join the gathering.
A : What a great idea! Thanks. When should I be there?
B : You can come around 6 o'clock.
A : All right then. See you on Saturday.
B : Great! I'll be expecting you.

wonder : 궁금해하다, 알고싶어 하다
family gathering : 가족 모임
What do you have in mind?(= What do you want to do?) : 무엇을 생각하고 있니?
go to the cinema : 영화 보러 가다
available : 시간이있는, 여가가 있는
It sounds like fun : 그거 참 재미있게 들리는데
unfortunately : 유감스럽게도
pick up : (차로 사람을) 태우다, 마중 나가다
prepare : 준비하다
That's fine : 괜찮아, 문제없어, 좋습니다
mind : 신경쓰다, 마음에 꺼려하다 (대체로 의문문이나 부정문에 쓰인다)
delighted : 아주 기뻐하는
What a great idea! : 훌륭한 생각이야, 대단한 생각이야
Great! : (구어) 훌륭한, 신나는, 대단한
expect : 기대하다, 기다리다

Useful Words and Expressions

1) Sentence Examples

How many people are (there) in your family?	– There are four people in my family.
Is your family big?	– No, we have a small family.
Do you have any grandparents?	– I only have a grandfather.
What does your sister do?	– She is an interior designer.
Do you have any siblings?	– Yes, I have two brothers.
How old is your mother?	– My mother is 51 years old.
Is your brother working?	– Yeah, he is an engineer.
Are you close to your family?	– Yes, we're very close.
Do you spend much time with your parents?	– Not really. I prefer to spend time with friends.
Is your sister married?	– Yes, she is married with two kids.
So, do you have any nephew or niece?	– I just have one nephew, and he is so cute.

2) Make sentences out of the words below.

1. There / five people / are / in my family.

   _____

2. How / you / many / cousins / do / have?

   _____

3. My father / is / teaches / and my mother / at school / a housewife.

   _____

3) Family Tree

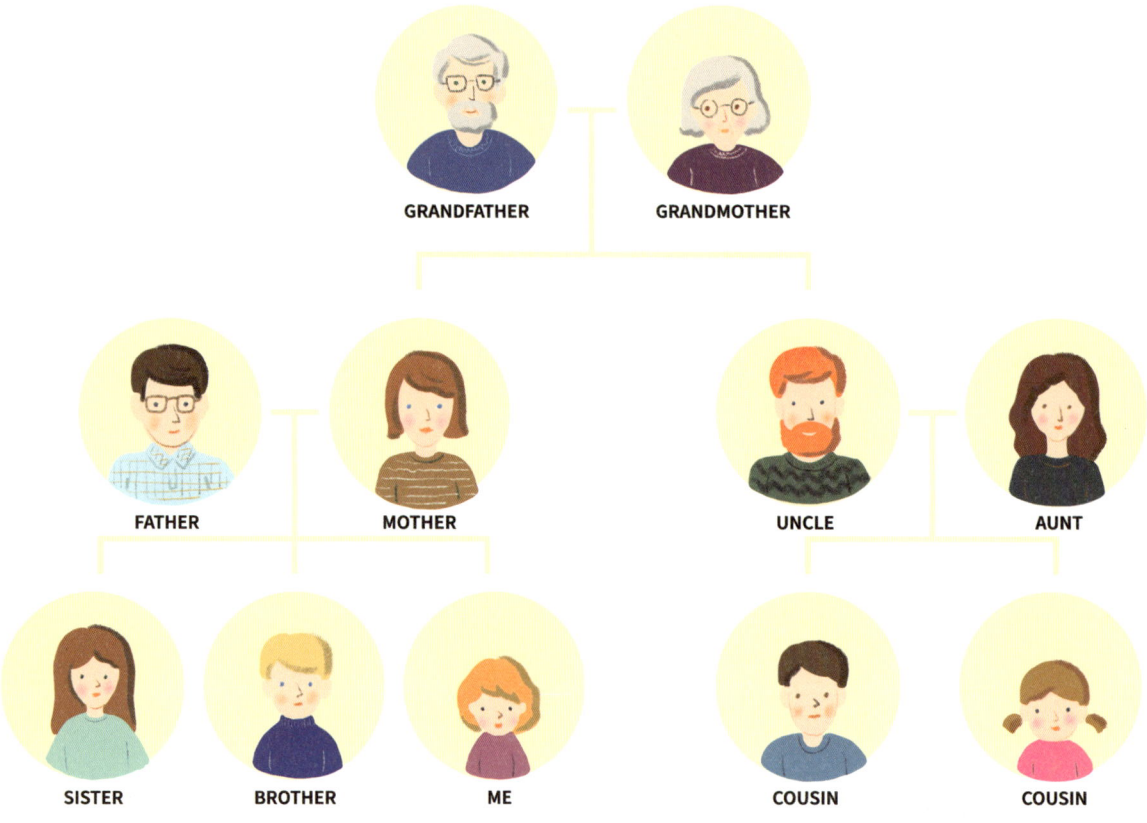

4) English Vocabulary Words for Family Members and Relatives

- grandfather, grandmother, grandson, granddaughter
- father, mother, father-in-law, mother-in-law
- husband, wife, ex-husband, ex-wife
- son, daughter, son-in-law, daughter-in-law
- brother, sister, half-brother, half-sister, stepbrother, stepsister
- uncle, aunt, cousin, nephew, niece

Reading Comprehension - The United Kingdom

When you ask young people, what do you know about the United Kingdom? Probably a lot of them would mention the famous book "Harry Potter." Harry Potter is a series of fantasy novels written by British author J. K. Rowling and is one of the most translated series of all time. The first book, "Harry Potter and the Philosopher's Stone," has been translated into over 74 languages. Since the release of the first novel, the books have found immense popularity and commercial success worldwide. They have attracted younger readers as well as a wide adult audience and are often considered cornerstones of modern young adult literature. Harry Potter is the boy who lived, singled out by Lord Voldemort at birth to be his greatest rival, and our hero. Edinburgh Castle in Scotland, which is the background of the books, is the most recognizable landmark that dominates the city skyline. The beautiful old town of Edinburgh has remained in its original form over the years and was listed as a UNESCO Heritage Site. Scotland is a country that is part of the UK and has a unique Scottish culture.

immense popularity and commercial success : 엄청난 인기와 상업적인 성공
cornerstone : 기초, 긴요한 것
singled out : 발탁되다, 선발되다
recognizable landmark : 알아볼 수 있는 건축물, 획기적인 큰 건물
dominate : 위압하다, 우위를 차지하다

Conversation Practice

Please write your answers and practice with your partner.

Q1. Who is the oldest person alive in your family?
   Do you have grandparents?
   Do you have a grandfather or grandmother?

Q2. How many people are in your family?

Q3. Could you describe what your family is like?

Q4. How many siblings do you have, and what are they like?

Q5. Do you look more like your mom or your dad?

Q6. Do you think big or small families are better? And why?

Q7. What is your favorite family activity and why?

Q8. Who is your favorite relative?

Unit 03 Hobby

"What do you do in your free time?"

"Challenges are what make life interesting and overcoming them is what makes life meaningful."
- Joshua J. Marine -

Dialogue 1

A : What do you usually do in your spare time?

B : I like watching football on TV. Tottenham Hotspur is my favorite football club because I like Son Heung-Min. He is still young but doing very well, and I think he is quite good-looking as well. I envy him for his talent. What about you?

A : I play baseball with friends almost every weekend. Do you want to watch a baseball game with me this Sunday? I've got two tickets.

B : Have you? That sounds great. What team are you supporting?

A : I'm a big fan of the Doosan Bears.

B : That's a great team. They are doing exceptionally well this season. I am glad that I have a chance to watch their game. Let's go and cheer for them.

envy : 부러워하다, 질투하다
have와 **have got (=**'ve got)** : ......을 가지고 있다(현재형), 과거형은 동일하게 **had**이다.
- I have a new computer. 또는 I've got a new computer.
cheer for : 응원하다

Dialogue 2

A : What do you do when you are free?

B : My hobby is reading books. I love novels.

A : What is your favorite book?

B : My favorite book is "Harry Potter." I've read the whole series three times. What about you? What do you do in your free time?

A : I like to play computer games. My favorite computer games are "League of Legends" and "Battlegrounds." They are so much fun.

B : That's interesting. But you know, it's quite addictive.

A : I know. So I usually control myself, so that I don't spend too much time on it.

novel : 소설
addictive : 중독성이 있는

Dialogue 3

A : Hey, Sarah. What are you reading?
B : It's a movie magazine. I'm trying to find a good movie to watch.
A : I saw "Avengers" last night. It was great.
B : Oh, really? That's a big-budget action movie, isn't it?
A : Yeah, it's a superhero movie. There were a lot of fast and dynamic action scenes. It was really exciting.
B : Sounds interesting. What character do you like the most?
A : All the characters are interesting. Among them, my favorite is "Thor."
B : What do you like about him?
A : Well, although he is not from the earth, he joins the others to safeguard the universe. And he looks so cool with his hammer.

big-budget : 큰 비용이 들어간
fast and dynamic action scenes : 빠르고 역동적인 액션 장면들
safeguard the universe : 우주를 보호하다

Dialogue 4

A : What did you do during the summer vacation?
B : I studied for the TOEIC Test and also worked as a part-timer. What about you?
A : I went to China for five days with my family.
B : Oh yeah, how was it?
A : It was interesting. We went to see the Great Wall and the Forbidden City in Beijing. We had a wonderful time. But the weather was so hot and humid.
B : I didn't know Beijing could be so hot.
A : Me neither. It was so unbearable. But I love traveling, and I want to travel to as many countries as I can. Traveling is my hobby.

part-timer : 파트타임 직원
the Great Wall and the Forbidden City : 만리장성과 자금성
humid : (날씨, 공기 등이) 습기있는, 눅눅한
unbearable : 참기 어려운

Dialogue 5

A : Hi, Sarah, this is James. What are you doing?
B : Just watching TV at home. What's up?
A : Nothing much. Just chilling at home. I'm quite bored. I don't know what I'm going to do today, and it is only ten in the morning.
B : Me too. Do you think we are boring people?
A : I don't think we are boring. It's just that we don't have any hobbies.
B : That's right. What do you think we should do as a hobby?
A : That all depends on what you like to do. For example, I like to doodle on my notepad, so I'm thinking of doing some real drawings.
B : Well, I like to play the piano for fun.
A : That could be a good hobby.
B : Hobbies are never too late to learn. I'm going to make a list of all the things I like to do.
A : That's a good idea. I'm going to do the same.
B : I hope we can find something really interesting to do.

What's up? (= How are you? or What's happening?) : (구어) 무슨 일이니?
chill : 쉬다, 한가롭게 시간을 보내다
bored : (기분이나 감정의 상태를 표현) 지루한, 따분한
boring : (기분이나 감정을 유발하는 사람이나 사물을 표현) 지루한, 따분한
depend on : …. 에 달려있다, …. 나름이다
for example : 예를들어
doodle : 낙서하다
notepad : 노트패드 컴퓨터
drawing : 그림, 스케치
make a list : 명단을 작성하다
really : 정말로, 확실히
interesting : 흥미있는, 재미있는

Useful Words and Expressions

1) Sentence Examples

What is your hobby?	- My hobby is hiking.
What's your interest?	- I'm interested in music.
Do you watch TV?	- No, I seldom watch TV.
Do you like singing?	- Yes, I do. And I love to sing.
What kind of sports do you like?	- I like winter sports / water sports.
What is your favorite sport?	- My favorite sport is tennis.
What team are you supporting?	- I support Jeonbuk soccer team.
Do you like classical music?	- Not really. I prefer Jazz.
What's your favorite film?	- My favorite film is "Iron Man."
How often do you go to the movies?	- At least once a month.
What's your free-time activity?	- When I'm free, I play the guitar.
Do you exercise?	- Yes, I go to the gym everyday.

2) Make sentences out of the words below.

1. What / you / do / kind of movie / like?

   _____

2. I / outdoor sports / like / very much.

   _____

3. He / before breakfast / swimming / went / this morning.

   _____

4. Do / go for a run / you / every morning?

   _____

3) Hobby / Free-time Activity / Interest

- Hobby : a regular activity that is done for enjoyment.
- Free-time Activity : anything that you do when you are not working.
- Interest : an activity or subject which you enjoy doing or studying.

Different Activities

go to the movies	go hiking / mountain climbing
go to an amusement park	go jogging / running
go window shopping	go swimming / scuba diving
go dancing / clubbing	go sailing / surfing
boxing / wrestling / martial arts	go skiing / snowboarding
cooking / singing / traveling	work out at a gym
watch TV or videos	ride a bicycle / motorcycle
watch sports games	play volleyball / basketball
listen to music	play a musical instrument
read books	play chess / computer games
yoga / meditation	play with your pet (dog/cat)
hang out with friends	sleep all day

Reading Comprehension - China

China is the world's most populous country, occupying most of the entire East Asian landmass. The country occupies approximately one-fourteenth of the land area of the earth. There are many tourist attractions in China. However, when people go to China, the Great Wall is a great tourist destination for visitors and cannot be missed. It was built along an east-to-west line across the historical northern borders. As its name suggests, the Great Wall is the longest wall in the world, and it's often considered as one of the greatest man-made wonders. It was to protect the Chinese empires against the invasions of the various nomadic groups, and also served as a transportation corridor along the Silk Road. Several walls were built as early as the 7th century BC; these were later joined together, and made bigger and stronger. It was constructed over several centuries and claimed the lives of thousands of builders. But today the Great Wall of China stands out as one of the world's most famous landmarks.

populous : 인구밀도가 높은
the greatest man-made wonders : 위대한 인위적 불가사의들
northern border : 북방 국경(선)
invasions of the various nomadic groups : 다양한 유목집단들의 침략들
transportation corridor : 주요 수송경로
the lives of thousands of builders : 수천명 건축업자들의 생명들

Conversation Practice

Please write your answers and practice with your partner.

Q1. Have you got a hobby?
How long have you had your hobby?
How many hours a week do you spend on your hobby?
Are there any hobbies you would like to try?

Q2. What do you do in your free time?
What free-time activity do you do alone?

Q3. Do you like watching TV?
What kind of TV programs do you usually watch?

Q4. Do you play any sports? If you do, what's your favorite sport?
How often do you play?

Q5. Do you like to go to the movies?
What kind of movie do you like?
Who is you favorite actor/actress?

Q6. What do you usually do when you hang out with your friends?

Unit 04 School

"How many classes are you taking this semester?"

"If I had nine hours to chop down a tree, I'd spend the first six sharpening my axe."
- Abraham Lincoln -

Dialogue 1

A : Hello, Jane. What school do you go to, and what are you majoring in?
B : I go to Korea University, and I am majoring in Airline Service.
A : Which year are you in?
B : I am a freshman.
A : What's your favorite subject?
B : My favorite subject is English Conversation, but I'm not good in English Writing. I need to study harder to improve it.
A : What grade did you get for English Conversation last semester?
B : I got an A.
A : That's really good. You must be proud of yourself.
B : How many credits are you taking this semester?
A : I am taking 18 credits this time.

semester : 학기
credit (= unit / point) : 학점
be proud of oneself : .... 자신을 자랑스러워하다

Dialogue 2

A : Do you see your friends from primary school?
B : Not really. When I was young, my family moved around several times because my father was a soldier.
A : You are better than me. I lived in India until I was 14 years old. So I have only few friends from my time at middle school.
B : Well, having many friends around is good, but having one true friend is even better. That's what I think.
A : I agree with you. That's why I cherish my friendship with my best friend Jane. We've been friends since our high school days.
B : Yeah, I think we should appreciate our friendship.

primary school / elementary school : 초등학교
cherish : 소중히 여기다
appreciate : (호의 등을) 고맙게 생각하다, 감사하다

Dialogue 3

A : Have you seen James?
B : Yeah, I saw him at the library.
A : What was he doing there?
B : He was studying. He said, he has a big test tomorrow.
A : What about you? Where are you going?
B : I am going to the BTS concert with some friends.
A : Wow! How exciting, I love BTS. How did you get the tickets? I heard the tickets were all sold out a long time ago.
B : I know, we were lucky. I am a big fan of BTS.
A : Me too. I wish I could go. Have a good time anyway. I think I'd better do my homework tonight. We have to hand in the homework by this Friday.

I'd better (= had better) + 동사원형 : 나는 .... 하는 것이 좋겠다
hand in (= submit) : 제출하다
I wish I could go : (가정법 현재) 내가 갈 수 있다면 좋을텐데

Dialogue 4

A : You look so happy, what's the good news?
B : The semester is almost over, and summer vacation is coming.
A : So what are you going to do during the vacation?
B : I'm planning a trip to Africa for volunteer work.
A : Oh really? What will you do there?
B : I'll teach English to young local children. They are poor and can't afford to go to school.
A : What made you decide that?
B : I once read a story about "Father Lee Tae-Seok," and I was so impressed by his love and dedication to the poor people in Africa.
A : I know him too. He was a great man. I am sure your vacation will be very meaningful. Tell me about it when you come back. Have a good trip.

dedication : 헌신
meaningful : 의미 있는, 뜻깊은

Dialogue 5

A : Hi, Tom. What are you doing here? You look quite frustrated. Are you okay?
B : My Korean isn't perfect. And I'm having a hard time doing my homework. This is too hard. Can you help me with my homework?
A : I can understand how you feel. I have some time now. I'll help you.
B : Thanks, Jane. I'll treat you to lunch.

(After a while)

B : It's lunch time now. So shall we go have lunch?
A : Do you know what time our next class begins?
B : I think it starts at 1:30.
A : Oh! We only have less than an hour. How about we go to the cafeteria? Since it's nearby.
B : Okay. Let's go and just grab some sandwiches. Ooops! I think I forgot my wallet.
A : So you don't have money then?
B : No. Could you lend me some?
A : Sure. Here you are.
B : Thanks. I appreciate it. I'll pay you back tomorrow.
A : No problem. That's what friends are for.

frustrated : 좌절감을 느끼는, 불만스러운
hard time : 어려움
hard : 하기 힘든, 어려운
treat : 대접하다, ... 에게 한턱을 내다
less than an hour : 한시간보다 더 적은
cafeteria : 카페테리아, 구내식당
nearby : 가까운, 가까이의
grab : 급히 잡다, 잡아채다
wallet : 지갑
then : 그러면, 그렇다면
lend : (돈을) 빌려주다
pay back : (빌린 돈을) 갚다
That's what friends are for : 그런게 친구니까, 친구란 그런거니까

Dialogue 6

A : How was the English class this morning?
B : It was interesting. Where were you?
A : I overslept and missed the 8 o'clock school bus. And I've just arrived.
B : What's the matter with you?
A : I know, I'm so angry with myself too. Well, there was the World Cup game between Korea and Germany last night. As you know, I am crazy about soccer and couldn't miss the game.
B : What time did it start?
A : The game started at 1:00 a.m. and finished after 3:00 a.m. this morning.
B : Which team won?
A : Amazingly, Korea won. I was so thrilled.
B : So glad to hear that.
A : By the way, do we have any assignments to do?
B : Yes, we do. We have to submit an essay on foreign culture by next Tuesday.
A : I see. Thanks for the information.

oversleep : 늦잠자다
miss : (탈 것을) 놓치다, (... 할 것을) 놓치다
What's the matter with you? : 무슨 일이야? (책망하여) 어떻게 된거야?
angry : 화난, 화가난
be crazy about : .... 을 아주 좋아하다, ... 에 푹 빠져있다
soccer : 축구
amazingly : 놀랍게도
thrilled : 흥분한, 감격한
glad : 기쁜, 반가운
assignment (= homework) : 과제, 숙제
submit : 제출하다
essay : 에세이, 수필

Useful Words and Expressions

1) Sentence Examples

Do you go to a college?	– Yes, I'm a college student.
How long is your degree course?	– Two years.
What are majoring in?	– My major is Tourism.
What class do you like the most?	– English is my favorite subject.
How do you go to school?	– By school bus.
Is your university large or small?	– Our school campus is quite large.
Do you have many friends in school?	– Yes, I have a lot of friends.
Who is your close friend?	– My close friend is Tom.
When do you usually come home?	– I often come back late.
What time do you go to school?	– Usually, at around 8 o'clock.
Do you wear a uniform at school?	– Yes, we do.
How long is your lunch break?	– Just one hour.
What high school did you graduate from?	– I graduated from Seoul high school.
When did you graduate?	– I graduated last year / in 2019.

2) Make sentences out of the words below.

1. Have / finished / you / your homework?

   _____

2. Richard / to study / go to college / wants to / economics.

   _____

3. Do / our class / you / starts / what time / remember / tomorrow?

   _____

3) General School Types

- kindergarten / preschool
- primary school / elementary school
- middle school
- high school
- college / university

4) Majors

History	Airline Service	Fine Art
English Literature	Tourism	Architecture
Law	Chemistry	Engineering
Economics	Physics	Interior Design
Philosophy	Biology	Computer Science
Psychology	Medicine	Accounting
Sociology	Hotel Management	Mathematics

5) Grades

freshman – sophomore – junior – senior

6) Classroom Expressions

Come to class	Pay attention	Don't be shy
Take a seat	Listen carefully	Speak a little louder
Call / Take (the) roll	Repeat after me	Keep your book closed
Stand up	Read out loud	Turn to page 58
Raise your hand	Try again	Open your books to page 12

Reading Comprehension - Sudan

Most people nowadays are only concerned about their own interests, such as wealth, social status, and success; this tendency can sometimes cause problems in society. However, this is not the case with everybody. There is an appropriate person to take for example, Father Lee Tae-Seok, the priest known as "Korea's Schweitzer." Father Lee was born to a poor Korean couple. With passion, he went to Tonj, South Sudan to work for the poor, sick, and vulnerable in hopes to preach the spirit of sharing and sacrifice. Besides being a doctor and a priest, he was also a musician who helped start a local band for young people in the community. He taught the children mathematics and music, and treated the locals as if they were his best friends. At the age of forty eight, he died of cancer, and the news of his death was an astonishment and sorrow to many. Little may be known about Father John Lee Tae-Seok to most people in Africa, but the war-torn natives in Tonj will never forget him for his life of sacrifice, humility, and dedication.

appropriate : 적절한
vulnerable : 보호가 필요한
astonishment and sorrow : 놀람과 슬픔
war-torn native : 전쟁으로 피폐한 토착민

Conversation Practice

Please write your answers and practice with your partner.

Q1. What university do you go to?
    Which year are you in?

Q2. What is your major?

Q3. How many courses are you taking this semester?

Q4. What is your most interesting class?
    What subject do you like the most?

Q5. Do you get a lot of homework?

Q6. How often do you go to the library?

Q7. Do you enjoy your school life?
    What do you like and dislike about it?

Q8. What did you do during the last vacation?

Unit 05 Travel

"We'd like to go on a tour tomorrow."

"Life isn't about getting and having, it's about giving and being."
– Kevin Kruse –

Dialogue 1 - Travel Plan

A : I'm wondering if you would be able to help me with vacation plans.
B : Have you chosen your destination?
A : No, I haven't. Actually, I don't know where I want to go yet?
B : Do you enjoy warm weather, or are you looking forward to a cooler vacation?
A : A nice temperature climate would be ideal for me.
B : Why don't you take a look at these brochures. These might help you make up your mind.
A : They all look nice.
B : Have you thought about how much you would like to spend on this vacation?
A : I just got a bonus and can spend up to three thousand dollars total.
B : Once you decide the destination, I'll help you with all your travel plans.

vacation plan : 휴가 계획
actually : 사실은, 실은
destination : 목적지
temperature : 온도
climate : 기후
take a look (= have a look) : (...을) (한번) 보다
ideal : 이상적인
brochure : 책자
make up one's mind : 결정하다, 결단을 내리다
spend : (돈을) 쓰다, 소비하다
bonus : 보너스, 상여금
up to (something) : (특정한 수준, 정도)까지
total : 총액, 합계
decide : 결정하다
travel plan : 여행 계획

Dialogue 2 - Flight Reservation

A : Asiana Airlines, Kim speaking. Can I help you?
B : I'd like to make a reservation to San Francisco.
A : When would you like to fly, ma'am?
B : On July 15th in the afternoon, please.
A : Which class would you like to travel? First, Business or Economy?
B : I'll take Business Class.
A : All right. Please hold on, I'll check for you. ..... We have some seats available on the flight at 3:00 p.m.
B : Perfect. I'll take it.
A : May I have your name and contact number, please?
B : I am Fiona Simpson, and my phone number is 6335-6003.
A : Could you spell your last name as it's written on your passport?
B : Sure. It's S-I-M-P-S-O-N.
A : Thank you, Ms. Simpson. Your reservation has been made for Flight 872 leaving for San Francisco on July 15th, Monday at 3:00 p.m.
B : Thank you very much.
A : Thank you for calling Asiana Airlines and have a nice day.

(Kim) speaking : (전화를 받을 때) ....입니다
 - Who is speaking? : 전화를 받는 분은 누구입니까?
make a reservation : 예약하다
fly : 비행기로 날다, (특정 항공사를) 이용하다
hold on : (전화상으로 상대방에게 하는 말로) 기다리세요
I'll check for you : 확인해 드리겠습니다
available : 가능한
flight : 비행기 여행, 항공편
perfect : 완벽한, 최적의
contact number : 연락처 전화번호
Ms. : (혼인 여부에 상관없이 여성의 성 성명 앞에 붙여) ... 씨, 성과 함께 사용되거나 여성의 전체 이름과 함께 사용되는 호칭이다.
leaving for (= heading for / bound for / going to) : ....로 향하는 / 떠나는
Thank you for calling : 전화해 주셔서 감사합니다
have a nice day : 좋은 하루가 되세요

Dialogue 3 - Sightseeing

A : We'd like to go on a tour tomorrow. Do you have any recommendation for us?
B : Would you like to take the city tour or the boat tour?
A : Um..... Which one is better?
B : Well, the city tour is longer, but the boat tour can be more interesting.
A : Do you know what we can do on each tour?
B : Here are the brochures. Please have a look.
A : How much is the city tour?
B : It's ₩50,000 for each person.
A : How long is the tour?
B : It's a half-day tour, and you'll be back by 12:30 p.m.
A : What time does it start?
B : 9 o'clock in the morning.

recommendation : 추천

Dialogue 4 - Renting a car

A : I want to rent a mid-size car for two days. What's the rate?
B : Our daily rate is $38 plus tax.
A : Can you tell me what is included in that rate?
B : It includes insurance, gas, and unlimited mileage.
A : I see, that's fine.
B : When do you need it?
A : Tomorrow.
B : Would you like to pre-pay for the gas, or fill it up after?
A : I'll pre-pay for the gas now.
B : Can I have your driver's license, credit card, and passport, please?
A : Here they are.
B : The car will be ready in the parking lot tomorrow.

rate : 가격, 요금
insurance : 보험

Dialogue 5 - Business Trip

A : Hello, is this Korea Travel Agency?
B : Yes, it is. What can I do for you?
A : I'm planning to go to the Annual Exposition in Frankfurt, Germany. And I want you to help me with the trip.
B : I see. We can arrange flight and hotel reservations, and transportation for you. When do you want to go?
A : The first week of May.
B : And how many people will there be?
A : Just one person.
B : How long do you want to go for?
A : For five days. Could you please provide me the details?
B : If you leave your name and telephone number, I'll inform you about details of the trip as soon as possible.
A : My name is Oliver Thorn, and you can reach me at 2747-8855.
B : Thank you for choosing us, Mr. Thorn. I'll call you back soon.
A : Okay. Thanks a lot.

travel agency : 여행사
Annual Exposition : 연례 박람회
trip : 여행, 출장
arrange : 준비하다, ...의 예정을 세우다, (미리) 정하다
hotel reservation : 호텔예약
transportation : 차량, 차편, 이동방법
provide : 제공하다
details : 상세한 설명, 세부사항들
leave : 남기다
as soon as possible : 가능한 한 빨리
reach : ....에 닿다, (전화로) 연락하다
choose : 선택하다, 고르다
call back : (전화를 해 왔던 사람이나 누구에게) 다시 전화를 하다

Useful Words and Expressions

1) Sentence Examples

What country would you like to visit?	– The country I'd like to visit is Italy.
What's your budget for the trip?	– About two thousand dollars.
When do you want to fly?	– On November 11th.
Who do you like to travel with?	– With my friends.
How long will you be staying?	– For ten days.
How often do you travel?	– Well. …. I think, once a year.
So, where did you go last year?	– I went to Thailand.
How much is the boat tour?	– ₩80,000 per person.
How long will you rent this car for?	– Just for one day.
Why do you want to travel?	– Because it broadens my horizons.
Do you have any suggestion?	– I recommend you the DMZ tour.
Have you ever been to Africa?	– Yes, I've been to a few countries in Africa.
Which is better traveling alone or traveling with a group?	– I prefer to travel alone.

2) Make sentences out of the words below.

1. I / go on a tour / to Japan / want to / in November.

   _____

2. Oliver / to Turkey / is going on a trip / next month.

   _____

3. How long / the Atlantic / to cross / does it take / by ship?

   _____

4. Could / please / leave / you / your contact number?

   _____

3) Months

January	February	March	April	May	June
July	August	September	October	November	December

4) Dates

1st	first	11th	eleventh	21st	twenty-first
2nd	second	12th	twelfth	22nd	twenty-second
3rd	third	13th	thirteenth	23rd	twenty-third
4th	fourth	14th	fourteenth	24th	twenty-fourth
5th	fifth	15th	fifteenth	15th	twenty-fifth
6th	sixth	16th	sixteenth	26th	twenty-sixth
7th	seventh	17th	seventeenth	27th	twenty-seventh
8th	eighth	18th	eighteenth	28th	twenty-eighth
9th	ninth	19th	nineteenth	29th	twenty-ninth
10th	tenth	20th	twentieth	30th / 31st	thirtieth / thirty-first

Reading Comprehension - Brazil

Coffee is one of the most widely consumed beverages in Korea. Many people drink coffee at least once a day, and they don't mind spending more money for expensive brands like Starbuck's. With a café on every corner in many cities around the globe, it comes as no surprise that coffee is one of the top commodities worldwide. Brazil is responsible for about a third of all coffee, making Brazil by far the world's largest producer, a position the country has held for the last 150 years. Coffee plantations, are mainly located in the southeastern states where the environment and climate provide ideal growing conditions. There are two main commercially grown types of coffee beans, Arabica and Robusta which is far cheaper and easier to grow. Brazil is unrivaled in total production of green coffee, Arabica coffee, and instant coffee. Everyone loves talking about coffee - even if they don't drink it every day. If you're a lover of coffee, you might want to know who is delivering the most beans to market every year?

beverage : 음료
consume : 마시다, 소모하다
commodity : 상품, 필수품, 일용품
plantation : 대규모 농장
unrivaled : 경쟁자가 없는

Conversation Practice

Please write your answers and practice with your partner.

Q1. What was the first trip that you remember taking?

Q2. How many countries have you visited?
    Is it better to go on a package tour or to travel by your own?

Q3. Who would you like to take a trip with?

Q4. How do you like to travel when going on a trip?
    By car, train, bus, boat or airplane?

Q5. Have you ever been sick while travelling?

Q6. Where do you want to go on your next trip?
    What's your next destination?

Q7. What was the furthest you've ever traveled from home?
    Where's the farthest place you've ever traveled to?

Q8. Can you drive a car?
    Have you ever been in a car accident?

Unit 06 Airport

"How many bags would you like to check?"

"Love yourself first and everything else falls into line. You really have to love yourself to get anything done in this world."
– Lucille Ball –

Dialogue 1 - Ticketing

A : May I help you?
B : I'd like to purchase a ticket to Paris.
A : Did you make a reservation?
B : No, I didn't.
A : When would you like to fly?
B : On August 25th.
A : Which class would you like to take?
B : Economy class.
A : Would you like a round-trip ticket or one way ticket?
B : Round trip, please.
A : We have some seats available on the 7:00 p.m. flight.
B : That's good. I'll take it. How much is the fare?
A : It's $1,500 for a round-trip.
B : Okay. I'll take it.
A : How would you like to pay?
B : I'll pay by credit card. Do you accept Visa?
A : Yes, we do. Can I have your credit card, please?
B : Here it is.
A : May I have your signature here?
B : Right. ..... Here you go.
A : Thank you. You are all set. Have a pleasant day.

purchase : 구매하다
round-trip ticket (= return ticket) : 왕복 티켓
one way ticket : 편도 티켓
fare : 요금
accept : (신용카드를) 받아주다, 받다
credit card : 신용카드
Here it is / Here they are : 자, 여기 있습니다 (누군가에게 무엇을 주거나 보여줄 때)
signature : 서명, 싸인
You are all set : 다 됐습니다.
pleasant : 즐거운, 유쾌한, 기분 좋은

Dialogue 2 - At the Check-in Counter

A : Good morning. Can I have your passport and ticket, please?
B : Here you are.
A : Would you like an aisle seat or a window seat?
B : Er.... a window seat, please.
A : All right, ma'am. Do you have any baggage to check?
B : Just these two bags. And I'll carry this one myself.
A : Could you put your bags on the scale, please?
B : Sure. .... There you go.
A : Here are your boarding pass and baggage claim check. Your seat is 21A, and the boarding gate is 15. Boarding will begin at 10:30.

scale : 저울
baggage claim check : 수하물 영수증
boarding gate : 탑승구

Dialogue 3 - Immigration

A : Could I see your passport and disembarkation card, please?
B : Here you are.
A : Is this your first visit to the United States?
B : Yes, it is. I've never been here before.
A : Do you have any family or relatives in America?
B : No, I don't have any.
A : What is the purpose of your visit?
B : We are here on vacation. Our family is going to Disneyland.
A : How long do you intend to stay?
B : Just for one week.
A : And where will you be staying?
B : We'll be staying at the Marriot Hotel in Santa Monica.
A : Here are your papers. Have a good time.

immigration : 입국관리(심사)
disembarkation card : 입국신고서

Dialogue 4 - Customs

A : May I look at your passport and customs declaration form, sir?
B : Certainly. Here you are.
A : Do you have anything to declare?
B : No, nothing. Just the normal allowance.
A : Do you have any cigarettes or liquors?
B : Yes. I have one bottle of whiskey and two cartons of cigarettes.
A : OK then, could you please open your suitcase for me?
B : Sure.
A : What are those?
B : All these are my personal effects.
A : That's fine, thank you. You can proceed.

 customs declaration form : 세관신고서
 declare : (세관에서) 신고하다
 normal allowance : 보통의 허용량
 personal effects : 개인용품, 소지품
 proceed : 나아가다, 계속하다

Dialogue 5 - Baggage Claim

A : Excuse me. Can you tell me where I can collect my bags?
B : What flight did you arrive on?
A : Flight CX 889 from Vancouver, Canada.
B : You can get your baggage at carousel number 7.
A : How can I find that carousel?
B : Take the escalator and go downstairs. You'll see number 7 displayed on the signboard. It will also show the flight number and the place of origin.
A : Thank you so much.
B : You're welcome.

 carousel : 수하물 컨베이어 벨트
 signboard : 게시판, 표시판
 the place of origin : 출발장소

Dialogue 6 - At the Information Desk

A : Hello. How may I help you?
B : I want to exchange some money. Is there a bank or currency exchanger around here?
A : There is a bank over there on your right.
B : Oh, I see, thanks. ......
A : Do you need anything else?
B : Yes. I was wondering how I could get downtown from the airport?
A : We have buses and taxis. A taxi will cost around ₩50,000 to the city center depending on the traffic, and the Limousine bus will cost about ₩12,000.
B : How long does it take?
A : It depends, but I think the traffic will be quite light at this time of the day. So if you take the Limousine bus, you will get there in an hour. It's nonstop and the price is reasonable.
B : In that case, I'll take the Limousine bus. Thank you for all the information.
A : You're welcome. Have a pleasant stay in Korea.

currency exchanger : 환전상
traffic : 교통, 교통량
reasonable : (값 등이) 비싸지 않은, 적당한

Dialogue 7 - Currency Exchange

A : I'd like to change some US dollars into Korean won, please.
B : Certainly. How much would you like to change?
A : Could you tell me what the current exchange rate is?
B : It's ₩1,120 to one US dollar.
A : And do you charge a commission?
B : No, we don't.
A : In that case, I'll change 500 dollars.
B : Please sign here. .... Here is your receipt and your money.

currency exchange rate : 환율
commission : 수수료
receipt : 영수증

Useful Words and Expressions

1) Sentence Examples

Where should I check-in?	– Please go to counter No. 5.
What is the gate number?	– It's Gate 26.
When do you start boarding?	– In about 20 minutes, sir.
How many pieces of luggage do you have?	– I have two suitcases to check, and this is my carry-on luggage.
Please put your bags on the scale.	– Here you go.
Where is the baggage claim area?	– It's downstairs.
What is the purpose of your visit?	– I'm here on business.
How long will you stay in Australia?	– For two weeks.
Where are you going to stay?	– I'll be staying at the Plaza Hotel.
Do you have anything to declare?	– I have some foodstuffs from Korea.
Can I help you, ma'am?	– Yes. It seems my bags are missing.
Where is the information desk?	– It's outside.

2) Make sentences out of the words below.

1. Would / opening / you / mind / your briefcase?

    _____

2. We / to visit / are going to Toronto / some friends of ours.

    _____

3. Your luggage / to your next flight / will be / transferred / automatically.

    _____

4. Which seat / a window seat / would you prefer, / or an aisle seat?

    _____

Reading Comprehension - Russia

There are numerous programs on TV introducing many different countries in the world and how to travel. Some might choose to travel by plane, ship, train, bicycle or on foot. How about taking the Trans-Siberian train? It's the journey almost everyone wants to do, perhaps because it's commonly said to be the longest trip you can take on a single train. The longest of the three Trans-Siberian routes between Moscow and Vladivostok takes seven days. To enjoy longer hours of daylight and the chance of fine weather, it's best to go between May and September though it's cheaper during winter. The journey can be broken into sections with overnight stays in hotels. On the regular public trains, bedding is supplied; food quality is generally acceptable though menus are limited. Stops at stations allow food to be bought from platform vendors or shops, but always make sure you know how long each stop is before venturing far from the coach. Some are no more than five minutes, and people have been left behind. Since Russia is the world's largest country, it can be one way to discover the country's immense landscape.

be broken into sections : 구간들로 나누어지다
bedding : 침구
platform vendor : (기차역) 플랫폼의 행상인
venturing : 과감히 해보는 것

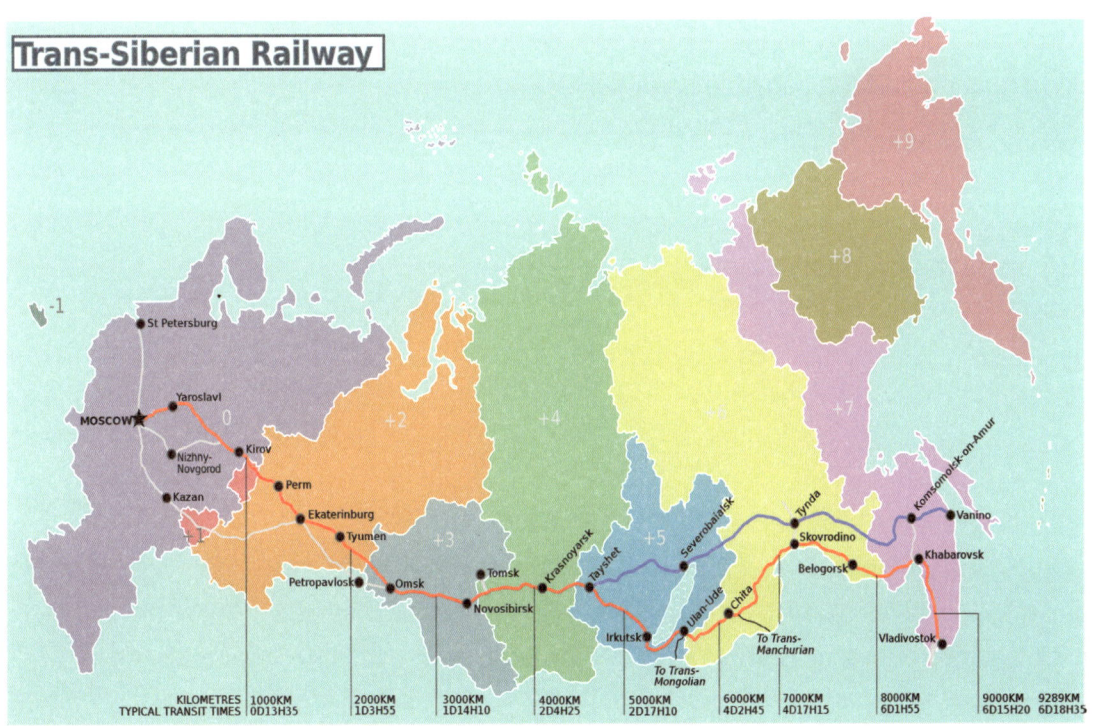

Conversation Practice

Please write your answers and practice with your partner.

Q1. Have you ever traveled abroad before?
If yes, where? And if no, where would you like to travel to?

Q2. Have you filled in your landing forms?

Q3. What is the purpose of your trip?

Q4. How long will you stay? / How many days will you be here?

Q5. Have you got anything to declare?

Q6. What was your flight number?

Q7. How can I collect my baggage? / Where can I pick up my bags?
Where can I find the baggage carousel?

Q8. Where is the information desk?

Unit 07 Airplane

"Would you please fasten your seat belt?"

"When everything seems to be going against you, remember that the airplane takes off against the wind, not with it."
– Henry Ford –

Dialogue 1 - Passenger Boarding & Seating Arrangement

A : Good afternoon, sir. Welcome aboard. May I see your boarding pass, please?
B : Yes, here you are.
A : Your seat number is 35C. The aisle seat right over there.
B : My wife and I were assigned separate seats. Is it possible to sit together?
A : I'll see if it can be arranged. Just a moment, please.
B : OK. Thanks.

(A little later)

A : Thank you for waiting. We have some empty seats at the back of the cabin. It's 56A and B. Would that be alright?
B : Yes, that would be fine as long as we can sit together.
A : This way, please ...... Here are your seats. You can stow your bag in the overhead compartment. Where is your wife?
B : She is in 45H.
A : I'll go and bring your wife here.
B : Thanks for your help.
A : My pleasure. If you need anything else during the flight, please let us know. Have a nice flight.

    boarding pass : 탑승권
    aisle seat : 복도 좌석
    right over there : 바로 저기입니다
    be assigned : 지정받다
    separate : 떨어진, 분리된
    empty : 비어있는, 빈
    sit together : 자리를 같이 앉다
    as long as : .... 하는한, ... 하기만 하면
    stow : 집어넣다, 싣다
    overhead compartment : 머리 위 선반 함
    bring : 데려오다
    anything else : 그밖에 또 무엇인가, 무슨 다른 것
    please let us know : 저희에게 알려주세요

Dialogue 2 - Meal Service

A : We'll be serving dinner soon. Would you please open the tray table?
B : What's the meal today?
A : We have Chicken Teriyaki, Shrimp Tempura, and Beef Steak. Which one would you like?
B : I'll have Chicken Teriyaki, please.
A : Here it is. Would you care for red or white wine?
B : Could I have a beer?
A : Of course. Do you have any preference?
B : I like Heineken. Do you have one?
A : Yes, we do. Here is your beer.
B : Thanks.
A : You're welcome. Enjoy your meal.

preference : 선호하는 것, 더 좋아함

Dialogue 3 - Flight Information

A : Excuse me. How long will it take us to get to New York?
B : The flight time is 13 hours.
A : What's the time difference?
B : New York is 14 hours behind Seoul. It's about 10 o'clock local time in the morning now.
A : Thanks. Is it Monday or Tuesday?
B : It's Monday, sir.
A : What time are we arriving in New York?
B : We're scheduled to arrive at 1:30 p.m. local time.
A : Thank you very much.
B : My pleasure. Enjoy your flight.

flight time : 비행시간
time difference : 시간차이
local time : 현지시간
be scheduled : ..... 할 예정이다

Dialogue 4 - C.I.Q. Information

A : Excuse me. I am staying in Korea for three days. Do I need to fill out these landing cards?
B : Yes, ma'am. All passengers entering Korea must fill in both immigration and customs forms except transit passengers.
A : I see.
B : Do you need some help filling in the forms?
A : No thanks. I think I'm all right.
B : If you have any questions, please let me know.
A : Okay. Thanks.

enter : .... 에 들어가다
fill out (= fill in) : 기입하다
landing form : 입국서식
except : .... 을 제외하고, ... 외에는
transit passenger : 환승 승객

Dialogue 5 - Inflight Sales

A : Would you like to buy some duty-free items?
B : What do you sell?
A : We have liquors, cigarettes, perfumes, cosmetics, and some gift items.
B : Um..... Can I have a bottle of Johnnie Walker Black, please?
A : Certainly, sir. Here you are. That'll be $50.
B : Here's one hundred dollars.
A : Sorry. I'm afraid I don't have change right now. Would you like to pay by credit card instead.
B : Do you accept American Express card?
A : Yes, we do.

liquor : 술, 증류주
certainly : (대답으로) 알았습니다, 물론이죠
change : 거스름돈, 잔돈
instead : 그 대신에

Dialogue 6 - Attending Sick Passengers

A : Excuse me. I'm not feeling well.
B : How do you feel, madam?
A : I feel dizzy and nauseous. I get airsick easily. Do you have any medicine for that?
B : Yes, we have some anti-airsickness medicine. Would that be alright?
A : Yes, please.
B : Just a moment. I'll get it for you right away.

(A little later)

B : Here's your anti-airsickness tablet, and some warm water for you. And this is an airsick bag just in case you feel like vomiting.
A : Thank you. Is there an empty row somewhere? So I can lie down.
B : I'm sorry, I'm afraid all the seats are occupied. We have a full flight today.
A : I see. ...... How do I recline my seat?
B : Just press this button and lean back. I'll bring you extra pillows and blankets. I hope you'll get better soon.

(After a while)

B : How are you feeling now? Do you feel any better?
A : I feel much better now.
B : Good. I'm glad to hear that. Can I get you anything else?
A : No thanks. I'm fine.

dizzy : 어지러운, 현기증 나는
nauseous (= nauseated) : 메스꺼운, 토할 것 같은
get airsick : 비행기 멀미가 나다
anti-airsickness medicine : 비행기 멀미약   airsick bag : 비행기 멀미 봉투
right away (= immediately) : 즉시, 곧
vomit : 구토하다
lie down : 눕다
I'm afraid .... (= I'm sorry, but ...) : 죄송하지만 (정중한 표현)
recline : (좌석을) 뒤로 젖히다
lean back : 뒤로 기대다

Dialogue 7 - Cabin Preparation

A : Excuse me, sir. May I collect your headset?
B : Here you are.
A : Would you mind keeping your bag under the seat, please?
B : Sure. I will.
A : And please return your seat back to the upright position and fold the tray table.
B : How can I return my seat to the upright position?
A : Please press the button and lean forward.
B : Okay, thanks. Are we descending now?
A : Yes, we are. We'll be landing shortly.

headset (= headphone) : 헤드폰
Would you mind + -ing형 : (상대방에 요구할 때) ... 해 주시겠습니까?
   - Would you mind opening the window?
return : 되돌려 놓다
seat back : 좌석 등받이
upright : 똑바로 선, 수직의
fold : 접다
tray table : (비행기 내의 개인용) 탁자, 테이블
press : (....을) 누르다
lean forward : 앞으로 굽히다
descend : 하강하다
land : 착륙하다
shortly : 곧, 얼마 안있어

Useful Words and Expressions

1) Sentence Examples

Can you help me with my luggage?	– Sure. I'll help you.
Where is my seat?	– It's 52K, window seat, sir.
May I have a can of beer?	– What kind of beer would you like?
Would you like some wine?	– Yes, a glass of red wine, please.
Anything else for you, sir?	– No, I'm fine.
Would you care for some coffee?	– Actually, I prefer tea.
When are you showing the movie?	– After the meal service, ma'am.
What kind of drinks do you have?	– We have liquors, juices, soft drinks, and beer.
Would you like to buy some duty-free items?	– I'd like to buy some cigarettes.
What time do we arrive in Rome?	– The arrival time is 6:20 a.m.
How long is the flight time?	– It's 5 hours 45 minutes.
Can I have an immigration card?	– Certainly, here you are.
Do I have to fill out this customs form?	– Yes, sir. All passengers entering Canada must fill in the form.
Please fasten your seat belt.	– Okay, I will.

2) Make sentences out of the words below.

1. How long / from Hong Kong / does it take to get / to Sydney?

    _____

2. It takes / from Seoul / to fly / about 11 hours / to Amsterdam.

    _____

3. Are / any vacant seats / there / at the back of the plane?

    _____

3) Different Types of Landing Form (C.I.Q.)

- Customs Form : 세관신고서
- Immigration Form : 입국신고서
- Quarantine Form : 검역신고서

4) General Service Etiquette in the cabin

Service etiquette is a code / norm of manner and behavior.

- Always serve the elderly first, followed by ladies, and then inner / window seat passengers.
- Face the passenger when serving.
- Inform passengers when presenting / serving / collecting items.
- NEVER ask the passenger near to you to pass the item on your behalf.
- NEVER pass any items over passengers or across the aisle.

Reading Comprehension - Spain

Football is one of the most popular sports in Spain. The Spanish are crazy about football, and it's almost like a religion to them. Their passion can be seen in the football games. Whenever the Spanish national team wins, people run to the streets to celebrate. And the team will hit the streets on a bus, celebrating together and thanking them for their support. The Spanish national team is full of stars, and it's not easy to choose the best ones. Even the players on the bench are great players from teams like Real Madrid or Barcelona. "El Clásico" or "The Classic" is the name given to any match between Real Madrid and FC Barcelona; it features famous soccer players such as Messi, Ronaldo, Casillas, Valdes, Benzema, Xabi, and more. This is a clash of two soccer giants where incredible goals are frequently scored, and where tempers flare so frequently; it is not uncommon to see red cards given. Heroes are made in this game, and sometimes so are villains. There is a famous Spanish saying, *"Sin prisa, sin pausa,"* which means "Don't hurry, but don't stop." What about you?

be full of : ..... 이 많다, 가득차다
feature : 특별히 포함하다, 특색으로 삼다
clash : 충돌, 격돌
incredible : 놀라운, 대단한, 굉장한
temper : 성질, 기분
villain : 악한, 악인

Conversation Practice

Please write your answers and practice with your partner.

Q1. Would you like another cocktail?
Would you care for any other drink?

Q2. Could you open your tray table, please?

Q3. We have beef, chicken, and fish. Which one would you prefer?

Q4. Have you finished with your meal?
May I collect your tray?

Q5. Would you care for some coffee or tea?
How would you like your coffee?
Would you like some lemon with your tea?

Q6. Can I get you something else? How about some salad?

Q7. How long does it take to fly from Los Angeles to New York?
How long did it take? / How long will it take?

Q8. May I take your order for duty-free items?

Unit 08 Hotel

"I'd like to reserve a room for this weekend."

"Happiness is not something ready made. It comes from your own actions."
– Dalai Lama –

Dialogue 1 - Reception (Reservation)

A : Good afternoon. The Sheraton Hotel, James speaking. How may I best assist you? (formal greeting)
B : I want to make a reservation, please.
A : Certainly. When are you planning to stay?
B : It will be from 15th to 17th of October.
A : For two nights, sir?
B : That's right.
A : What kind of room would you like? Single or double?
B : I need a double room.
A : Just a moment, please. ..... I'll check for you.
B : And also, would it be possible to have a room with a sea view?
A : Sure, I'll just check what we have available. ...... Yes, we have a room on the 6th floor with a really splendid view.
B : Great. How much is the charge per night?
A : It's 150 euro per night excluding VAT.
B : It's fine.
A : Who is the booking for?
B : Mr. and Mrs. Simpson.
A : Alight, let me make sure I got that: Mr and Mrs Simpson. Double room for October 15th to 17th. Is that correct?
B : Yes, it is. Thank you very much.
A : Thank you for choosing the Sheraton Hotel and have a nice day. Goodbye.

    double room : (호텔 등의) 2인실
    Just a moment : 잠시만요
    splendid view : 훌륭한 전망, 경치
    charge : 요금
    per night : 하루밤에
    excluding : 제외한
    VAT (Value Added Tax) : 부가세
    euro (= €) : European Union(EU)의 화폐단위
    make sure : ....을 확실하게 하다
    correct : 정확한, 틀림없는

Dialogue 2 - Reception (Special Request)

A : Good morning. The Regent Hotel, may I help you?
B : Hello. I'd like to reserve two rooms for my family for a week.
A : Certainly, sir. When will you be arriving?
B : We'll be driving up on Wednesday morning.
A : Please hold the line, let me check. ..... Yes, we have rooms available on that day. Do you have any special requirements?
B : Yes, my son is in wheelchair.
A : No problem, sir. We have a room that will suit your needs. It also has a beautiful mountain view. You'll like it.
B : Good. We have a special van. Will there be a problem for parking?
A : No, sir. You'll have a reserved spot right outside the door, and the room is located beside the elevator.
B : Excellent.

    reserve a room : 방을 예약하다
    drive up : 자동차로 오다
    hold the line : 끊지말고 기다리십시오
    special requirement : 특별한 요구
    No problem : 문제 없습니다
    suit : (목적, 조건 등에) 적합하다, 맞다
    need : 요구, 필요
    special van : 특별한 밴 (운반차량)
    reserved spot : 지정된 장소
    locate : (특정 위치에) 두다, 위치하다
    Excellent : 아주 좋아, 정말 잘 됐어 (기쁨, 흡족함을 나타냄)

Dialogue 3 - Reception (Check-in)

A : Good afternoon, sir. How can I be of service? (formal greeting)
B : Yes, I'd like to check in, please.
A : Have you made a reservation?
B : Yes. I have a reservation under the name of Simpson.
A : Please wait a moment while I check our reservation list. ..... Yes, we have. Would you please fill in this registration card?
B : Right. ...... Here you go.
A : Thank you Mr. Simpson. Your room number is 312. Here is your key card. The bellboy will take your bags and show you to your room.
B : Thank you.
A : Please enjoy your stay.

    be of service (to somebody) : (…에게) 유용하다, 도움이 되다
    under the name of : ..... 의 이름으로, ... 명의로
    registration card : (숙박 절차로서 필요한 사항을 기재하는) 등록카드
    bellboy (= bellhop) : 벨보이 (호텔에서 손님들의 짐을 운반하는 사람)

Dialogue 4 - Laundry

A : This is laundry service. Can I help you?
B : I have some shirts to be cleaned, and pants to be ironed. Can you send someone over to my room?
A : Certainly, sir. May I have your name and room number, please?
B : I am Paul Simpson in room 312. How soon can I get them back?
A : It will be ready by tomorrow.
B : Is it possible to have them back this evening? I need to wear them for dinner.
A : Very well, sir. We have an express service. We'll try our best to deliver them to you by 6 p.m. today.

    send over : 보내다, 파견하다
    get back : 되찾다, 돌려받다
    express service : 특급서비스, 빠른 서비스

Dialogue 5 - Housekeeping

A : Housekeeping. How can I assist you?
B : This is room 513. The power suddenly went out, what's wrong with it?
A : Is that right? Did you insert your key card in the key slot?
B : Yes, I did.
A : Are you using any electric appliances?
B : I was only using the coffee pot.
A : Oh, I see. Maybe it caused some short circuit problem. We'll have it examined and taken care of right away.
B : It's so dark here. Please send someone up as soon as possible.

    electric appliance : 전기 제품(기구)
    short circuit : 단락(短絡), 누전, 합선
    have it examined : have는 사역동사로, 그것을 조사/검사하다
      – **have** + **목적어** + **과거분사** : 목적어가 어떤 상태가 되게 만든다는 수동의 의미
    send (somebody) up : (사람을) 올려보내다

Dialogue 6 - At the Bar

A : Good evening! Would you care for a drink?
B : Yes. I'll have a double scotch.
A : Is that straight up or on the rocks?
B : On the rocks, please.
A : How about you, sir?
C : A gin and tonic, please.
A : I'll be right back with your drinks.

(A little later)

A : Here are your drinks. And some potato chips on the house. Enjoy your drinks.

    straight up : (위스키, 칵테일 등이) 얼음이 없이 나오는
    on the house : (술집, 식당에서) 무료로 제공되는, (비용을) 주최자 부담으로

Dialogue 7 - Room Service

A : Good morning! Room service. How may I help you?
B : Hello. I'd like to order some breakfast, please.
A : Certainly, madam. What kind of breakfast would you like to have?
B : I'd like to have an English breakfast.
A : What kind of juice would you like with that? We have orange juice, tomato juice, and grapefruit juice.
B : I'll have an orange juice, please.
A : Would you prefer coffee or tea?
B : Tea, please.
A : And how do you like your eggs?
B : I'd like scrambled eggs and some toast, please.
A : Thank you madam. Your breakfast will be delivered to your room in about fifteen minutes.

English breakfast / American breakfast vs. Continental breakfast
주로 주요리(e.g. 달걀, 소세지, 베이컨 등)가 있냐, 없냐의 차이

Dialogue 8 - Reception (Check-out)

A : Good morning, sir. How are you today?
B : Very good. I'd like to check out now. My name is Simpson, room 312.
A : Did you have anything from the minibar?
B : No, I didn't.
A : One moment, please. ..... Here's your bill. Would you like to check and see if the amount is correct?
B : Sure. ...... Here is my credit card.
A : Thank you. Did you enjoy your stay?
B : Yes, the room was comfortable. Could you call a taxi for me, please?
A : Of course. Where are you going, sir?
B : I'm going to the airport.

check out : 체크아웃, (호텔의) 방을 비우다
minibar : (호텔 객실의) 소형 냉장고

Useful Words and Expressions

1) Sentence Examples

What kind of room would you like?	- I'd like to have a twin room.
How long will you be staying here?	- For three nights.
When is your arrival date?	- I'll be arriving on October 10th.
Can I have a wake-up call, please?	- Certainly, what time do you want?
Please fill out the registration card.	- Sure. …. Here you go.
How much is the charge per night?	- It's 200 dollars plus tax.
Do you have a swimming pool?	- Yes, it's on the third floor.
My room is dirty. Could you possibly clean the room now?	- I'm sorry, sir. I'll contact our housekeeping right away.
When is the check out time?	- It's 11 o'clock.
I'd like to check out, please.	- What's your room number, sir?
How would you like to pay?	- I'll pay by credit card.
What hotel will you be staying at?	- At the Four Seasons.

2) Make sentences out of the words below.

1. The hotel / was / we stayed at / near the beach.

   _____

2. I'd like / hotels / about / some information / in New York.

   _____

3. The room was / and everyone was / comfortable / very friendly.

   _____

4. May / your luggage / I / put / on the table, sir?

   _____

3) Hotel Room Types

Single Room	A room assigned to one person
Double Room	A room assigned to two people
Twin Room	A room with two beds, maybe occupied by one or more people
Suite	A class of accommodations with more space than a typical hotel room under one room number

4) How to order your eggs for breakfast?

- fried eggs : sunny-side up or over-easy
- scrambled eggs
- boiled eggs
- poached eggs

5) Hotel Services

Reception	books rooms for guests and answers their questions
Housekeeping	responsible for cleaning and checking guests' bedrooms
Room service	provides food and drink to guests in their rooms
Laundry	washes and irons clothes for guests

Reading Comprehension - Indonesia

If you are thinking about having a relaxing holiday, Bali can be on your destination list. Bali is an island located on the east of Java and west of Lombok. The island is surrounded by coral reefs. Beaches in the south tend to have white sand while those in the north and west have black sand. Being just eight degrees south of the equator, Bali has a fairly even climate all year round. After musician David Bowie died, his will revealed that Bowie asked for his ashes to be scattered in Bali, in accordance with the Buddhist rituals. Unlike most of Muslim-majority Indonesia, most Balinese believe in Hinduism. Its culture is strongly influenced by Indian, Chinese, and particularly Hindu culture. In terms of income, tourism is the largest single industry in this island; as a result, Bali is one of Indonesia's wealthiest regions. It is famous for its attractive surroundings, diverse tourist attractions, excellent international and local restaurants, and the friendliness of the local people. Bali was named as the World's Best Destination in the prestigious Trip Advisor Travelers' Choice Award.

coral reef : 산호초
equator : 적도
scatter : 흩뿌리다
Buddhist rituals : 불교도 의식
attractive surrounding : 매력적인 주변 환경

Conversation Practice

Please write your answers and practice with your partner.

Q1. Do you have any rooms available tomorrow? /
    Have you got any vacancies for tonight?

Q2. What kind of room would you like?
    Do you want a single or double room?

Q3. Would you like a room with bath or shower?

Q4. Would you like a smoking or non-smoking room?

Q5. How long will you stay?
    How many nights will you stay?

Q6. How much is the room charge?
    What is the room rate?

Q7. How would you like to pay?
    Will you pay in cash or by credit card?

Q8. Do you have any special request?

Unit 09 Restaurant

"Are you ready to order, madam?"

"Your time is limited, so don't waste it living someone else's life."
- Steve Jobs -

Dialogue 1

A : Have you thought about where you want to go for dinner on Friday for your birthday?
B : Hmm.... I don't really know where I want to go.
A : You know, we could search the restaurant review sites.
B : Excellent idea. Let's take a look.
A : What kind of food would you like to have on your birthday?
B : I like a lot of things, but Chinese or Japanese would be good.
A : This one, Ginza Japanese Restaurant looks good.
B : Oh, yes. I've heard of that one. Everyone I've spoken with says that it's great.
A : Would you like to go there then?
B : I think that would be a really good choice. Let's call and book a table.

search : 찾다, 조사하다
restaurant review site : 레스토랑 평론 사이트
What kind of food .... : 어떤 종류의 음식
book a table : 테이블을 예약하다

Dialogue 2

A : Good evening, Chez Leon Restaurant. Can I help you?
B : Hello. I'd like to book a table for dinner this evening.
A : For how many people, madam?
B : A table for four, please.
A : At what time?
B : Seven o'clock.
A : I'm sorry. It's Saturday, and we're pretty busy this evening. If you don't mind, we have a table for eight o'clock. Would that be alright with you?
B : I see. ...... That'll do.
A : Could I have your name, please?
B : Simpson.
A : Alright, Ms. Simpson. A table for four at eight o'clock. We'll be looking forward to seeing you. Goodbye.

Dialogue 3

A : Are you ready to order?
B : Well. ..... Everything looks good. What's your suggestion?
A : Let's see. ..... Would you like to try fish or steak? They come with French fries and green salad.
B : What kind of fish do you have?
A : Today, we have codfish and mullet. Both of them are very fresh.
B : OK. I'll have the codfish.
A : And for you, sir?
C : I'd like try your steak dinner.
A : All right. Would you like it rare, medium, or well-done?
C : Medium, please.
A : Would you care for something to drink before your meal?
C : We'll have a bottle of red wine. Thank you.

Are you ready to order? : 주문하실 준비 되었나요? 주문하시겠습니까?
suggestion : 제안
codfish : 대구   mullet : 송어과 생선
rare, medium, or well-done : 스테이크 굽기의 정도

Dialogue 4

A : Good evening. How are you today? May I take your order?
B : Yes, please. What are your today's specials?
A : Our specials of the day are Grilled Salmon and Fettuccine Pasta.
B : I'll have the Grilled Salmon, and my wife will have the Fettuccine Pasta.
A : May I bring something from the bar?
B : Do you have Champagne?
A : Of course, we do.
B : We'll have two glasses of Champagne, please.
A : Certainly. I'll be back with your drinks shortly.

today's special : 오늘의 특별요리
grilled : 구운, 그을린

Dialogue 5

A : Excuse me, I've been waiting for my entrée for more than twenty minutes. Why is it taking so long?
B : I'm sorry to have kept you waiting, sir. I'll go and check with the kitchen immediately.

(A little later)

A : Hello, this is not what I ordered. I ordered the steak, but your waiter gave me this chicken.
B : I'm terribly sorry. Let me take this one, and I'll bring your order to you. But I'm afraid, it may take a little while.
A : How long?
B : About 15 minutes.
A : Be sure to bring me the right one this time.
B : Certainly, sir. I do apologize for the mistake, and I'll double check your order.

   entrée : 앙트레, 서양요리의 정찬에서 식단의 중심이 되는 요리
   I am sorry to have kept you waiting : 기다리게 해서 죄송합니다
   keep + (somebody) + **-ing형** : keep은 ing형을 취하는 동사
    - Sorry to keep you waiting so long.
   immediately : 곧, 즉시
   terribly : 몹시, 굉장히
   order : 주문
   a little while : 잠시, 잠깐
    - Can I take a little while to think about it?
   be sure to + 동사 : (명령형으로) 반드시(틀림없이) .... 하여라
   the right one : 맞는 것, 정확한 것
    - He is the right one for the project.
   apologize : 사과하다
   mistake : 실수, 착오
   double check : 재확인하다

Dialogue 6

A : Did you enjoy your meal?
B : Yes, it was excellent. We enjoyed very much.
A : May I show you our dessert menu?
B : Yes, please.
A : Here you are.
B : They all look good. What's popular here?
A : Well, many people like Strawberry Cheesecake and Tiramisu. They are very delicious.
B : I think I'll try a piece of Strawberry Cheesecake.
A : Would you care for coffee or tea with your dessert?
B : I'll have some white coffee, no sugar, please.
A : And for you, sir?
C : No dessert for me, but I'd like a cup of espresso, please.
A : Very well, sir.

(After a while)

C : Excuse me. Can we have our bill please?
A : Sure. Would you like one check or separate checks?
C : One check is fine.
A : Certainly. I'll be right back with your check in a moment.

(A little later)

A : Here is your bill, and you can sign right here.
C : Here you go.
A : This is your receipt, sir. Thank you for dining with us.

excellent : 아주 훌륭한
popular : 인기있는, 평판이 좋은
delicious : 맛있는
bill (= check) : (식당의) 계산서, 청구서
 – One check or separate checks? : 계산을 같이 하시겠습니까, 따로 하시겠습니까?
be right back : 곧 돌아오다
dine : 식사를 하다

Useful Words and Expressions

1) Sentence Examples

What kind of food would you like to have on your birthday?	– I think, Chinese food would be good.
Where is the new fusion restaurant?	– It's on Hollywood Road.
Have you made a reservation?	– Yes, we have.
May I get you something to drink?	– Just some water, please.
Are you ready to order?	– No, we need some more time.
So, how did you like the restaurant?	– I thought it was very good.
What was your favorite dish?	– The Fish Curry was my favorite.
Would you care for some cheese?	– No thanks.
Can I get you anything else?	– No. All we need now is our check.
Did you enjoy our service?	– Yes, the service was excellent.
How late is the restaurant open?	– They close at 10 p.m.
How many guests will be in your party?	– We are a party / group of 8 people.
Can we have a table by the window?	– Wait a moment, please. Let me check for you.

2) Make sentences out of the words below.

1. Are / to order / ready / you / ma'am?

   _____

2. We'd like to / you / our aplogies / offer / for the trouble.

   _____

3. How / you / like / would / your steak, sir?

   _____

Reading Comprehension - Germany

If you are a beer lover, you may already know what's on in Germany in the month of October. The Oktoberfest is the world's largest beer festival held annually in Munich. It is a folk festival running from mid or late September to the first weekend in October, with more than six million people from around the world attending the event every year. During the event, large quantities of beer are consumed; there is also a wide variety of traditional foods available. A big band open-air concert takes place, and everyone participating in the festival becomes a bit German. Singing the beloved beer hall songs and dancing on the tables. One of the highlights is the parade where thousands of people dressed in traditional costumes walk through the streets of the city center. They are followed by marching musical bands, decorated horse carriages, floats of the breweries, flag-wavers, riflemen, oxen, cows, and goats. The Oktoberfest is an important part of Bavarian culture, having been held since the year 1810, and it is the highlight of Germany's festival calendar.

traditional costume : 전통의상
decorated horse carriage : 장식된 마차
floats of the breweries : 양조장들의 (축제 때 장식을 달아 끄는)이동식 무대차들
riflemen : 소총 연대병들

Conversation Practice

Please write your answers and practice with your partner.

Q1. What's the best restaurant you've ever been to?
Why did you like it?

Q2. Have you ever made a reservation for restaurants?

Q3. What is the cheapest place to eat that you know?
About how much is a meal? Where is it?
How often do you go there?

Q4. Do you have a favorite place that you would like to go for a special occasion?

Q5. What is your favorite fast food restaurant?
Where is it?

Q6. Do you prefer to eat at a restaurant or at home?
How often do you eat out?

Unit 10 Weather

"What kind of weather do you like?"

"Strive not to be a success, but rather to be of value."
– Albert Einstein –

Dialogue 1

A : Hi, Jane. What's the weather like, today?
B : Hi, mom. It's sunny and hot as usual Californian summer. But there's an 80% chance of light showers tonight.
A : Oh, really? That's good.
B : What about the weather in Seoul?
A : It's scorching hot here. The temperature went up to 38 degrees Celsius yesterday.
B : Was it? That's surprising. Don't go out much, mom. You may get sick.
A : I won't. Aren't you going to school today?
B : Yes, I have a class to attend this afternoon.

    scorching hot : 타는 듯이 뜨거운, 불볕더위의
    light showers : 가벼운 소나기
    Celsius / Centigrade vs. Fahrenheit
     - Celsius / Centigrade : 섭씨 (e.g. 0℃)   - Fahrenheit : 화씨 (e.g. 32℉)
    surprising : 놀라운, 의외의
    attend : (학교에) 출석하다

Dialogue 2

A : It's an ugly day today.
B : I know. I think it might rain.
A : It's the middle of summer, it shouldn't rain today. That would be weird.
B : Yeah, especially since it's 30 degrees outside.
A : I know, it would be horrible if it rained and it was hot outside.
B : Right, it would be.
A : I really wish it wasn't so hot every day.
B : Me too. I can't wait until winter.
A : I like winter too, but sometimes it gets too cold.
B : I'd rather be cold than hot.

    ugly : (날씨 등이) 험악한, 사나운
    weird : 이상한
    horrible : 끔찍한, 무서운

Dialogue 3

A : Good morning!
B : Morning. How are you today?
A : Am good, apart from all this rain. It's raining cats and dogs.
B : Yes, it's awful, isn't it? And it is very cold. The weather forecast said it will brighten up after lunch.
A : They always say that. Still, I can't complain, it's a lot warmer than back home.
B : Where are you from?
A : From Russia. Freezing cold and snowing.
B : I see. So this must be like summer for you.
A : Right. But I do like the snow sometimes.

    It's raining cats and dogs : 비가 억수로 내린다
    awful : (정도가) 대단한, 아주 심한
    weather forecast : 일기예보
    brighten up : 밝아지다, 환해지다
    complain : 불평하다
    freezing : 몹시 추운, 어는

Dialogue 4

A : Hey, Tom, it's a beautiful day, isn't it?
B : Yeah. I wish it would be like this everyday.
A : Do you know what the weather is going to be like tomorrow?
B : It's supposed to be the same as today. I don't think the weather will change much for the next week or so.
A : That's great.
B : Do you have anything planned?
A : Yeah, I'm going to Everland with my family this weekend, so I was hoping for good weather.
B : I'm so jealous of you. Have fun with your family.

    jealous : 시샘하는, 부러워하는

Dialogue 5

A : It's freezing outside.
B : Yeah, it's so cold, isn't it?
A : What happened to the weather report? I thought this cold front was supposed to pass.
B : I thought so too. That's what I read online this morning.
A : I guess the cold wind is really driving down the temperature.
B : I miss spring already. Spring time is really lovely here. I wish we could have that weather all year.
A : Don't say that. I don't want the earth to get any warmer. One of my classes yesterday got me worried about global warming.
B : I think we're all concerned about global warming. It's quite scary.

cold front : 한랭전선
global warming : 지구온난화
be concerned about : .....을 걱정하다, ...에 관심을 가지다
scary : 무서운, 두려운

Dialogue 6

A : Hi, do you want to go and get some lunch?
B : Yes, I'm getting hungry. Let's go.
A : I want to try the new café on the corner of Queen's Street.
B : Are you sure? It's very small, and we may have to sit outside.
A : That's why I want to go there. It's spring already, and the weather might be good for eating outside.
B : It looks as if it might rain soon. There has been some drizzle this morning.
A : No, the sky is clear, and you can see the sun.
B : But, it might be a bit chilly.
A : We can wear our coats. I want to sit in the sun for a while.
B : Okay, but if it starts to rain, we must go inside. Alright?

drizzle : 가랑비, 보슬비
a bit : 조금, 약간
chilly : 쌀쌀한, 차가운

Useful Words and Expressions

1) Sentence Examples

What's the weather like today?	– It's sunny and bright.
Isn't this weather miserable?	– Yes, it is. It's pouring down.
What's it like out there?	– Lovely day outside.
What was the weather like yesterday?	– It was quite chilly.
What was the temperature?	– It was 18 degrees Celsius.
Is the weather going to be good?	– I don't know. I have no idea.
What's the weather forecast?	– It will probably snow tomorrow.
What is your favorite type of weather?	– I like the weather, not too warm, not too cold.
What kinds of weather do you dislike?	– I would say, I really hate thunder and lightening.
Well, don't you think it's a beautiful day?	– Yeah. We couldn't ask for a better day than this.
So, what's the weather like in your city today?	– There's a mix of sun and clouds today.

2) Make sentences out of the words below.

1. Do you know / is going to be like / what the weather / next week?

   _____

2. It / since this morning / has been raining / and it's still raining.

   _____

3. The temperature / was / in Seoul / 33 degrees Celsius / yesterday.

   _____

3) English Vocabulary Words for Weather

hot	warm	cool	cold
sunny	dry	chilly	breezy
scorching	damp	cloudy	windy
nice	humid	misty	freezing
bright	drizzling	hazy	thundering
gloomy	rain	foggy	lightening
hazy	shower	snow	typhoon

Reading Comprehension - Turkey

Turkey is like a museum of human civilization that connects the East and the West. It spans the western part of Asia and Europe. Consequently, the culture and history of the East and the West are naturally intertwined, leaving various cultural remains. There are famous confections called "Turkish delight" or "Lokum." Turkish delight are small, fragrant cubes of jelly, and served with coffee or tea in the Middle East. The sweets are made by boiling sugar syrup and cornflour together slowly for several hours over a low heat. Lokum varieties include pistachios, chopped dates, hazelnuts or walnuts. They can be flavored with rosewater, orange blossom water, or lemon, and are presented in small cubes that are dusted with icing sugar to prevent them from sticking to each other. Turkish delight are known to have been produced in the country as early as the late 1700s, hence its name. Today people who travel to Turkey, it's a must-try.

human civilization : 인류문명
span : ..... 의 양끝을 연결하다
intertwine : 엉키다, 서로 얽히게 하다
remain : 유적, 유물
confection : 과자, 사탕 과자
hence : 이 사실에서 .... 이 유래하다
confection : 과자, 사탕 과자

Conversation Practice

Please write your answers and practice with your partner.

Q1. What do you think of the weather today?
What's the weather forecast for tomorrow?
Do you know what the weather forecast is like for this weekend?

Q2. Do you like going outside when the weather is good / bad?

Q3. What type of weather is most fun / miserable to you?

Q4. Do you like cold weather / hot weather?

Q5. When was the last time it rained / snowed?

Q6. Have you ever built a snowman?

Q7. Do you think meteorologists are good at forecasting the weather?

Q8. Are you concerned about global warming?

Unit 11 Directions

"Could you give me some directions?"

"Ask and it will be given to you; search and you will find; knock and the door will be opened for you."
- Jesus -

Dialogue 1

A : Excuse me, sir. Can you tell me how to get to Seoul station?
B : Do you want to take a bus or subway?
A : How long will it take by bus?
B : I think it may take about 40 minutes. But if you go by subway, it could be much faster.
A : My KTX train leaves at 11:30. I don't have much time.
B : In that case, you'd better take the subway.
A : Where is the nearest subway station?
B : The subway station is a five-minute walk from here. Go straight and make a left turn at the corner, and you will see the station.
A : Thank you very much for your help. I appreciate it.

get to a place (= arrive) : 도착하다
  - I usually get to school before 8:00. (= arrive at school)
  - We left Paris at 2:30 and got to New York at 5:00.
get home / here / there (without "**to**") :
  - What time did you get **home / here / there**?
you'd better (= you **had better**) : 당신은 ..... 하는 것이 좋겠습니다 (지시나 권고)
  - had better : 형태는 언제나 과거형으로 쓰나 의미는 가까운 미래 상황을 나타낸다
the nearest subway station : 가장 가까운 지하철역
a five-minute walk = five minutes' walk : 걸어서 5분 거리

Dialogue 2

A : Sorry to bother you. But I think we're lost. Can you direct us to the museum?
B : The museum? Go straight for two blocks.
A : Okay. After that, what do we do?
B : Then turn right and you'll see the post office. It's next to the post office. I'm sure you'll find it easily.
A : Thanks for the directions.

direct : 길을 알려주다   direction : (위치·이동의) 방향

Dialogue 3

A : Could you do me a favor?
B : Certainly. How may I help you?
A : Can you give me some directions, please?
B : What are you looking for, ma'am?
A : I want to go to the shopping center.
B : Are you driving or walking?
A : I think, I'd rather walk if it's not far.
B : Well, it's five blocks from here. It'll take about fifteen minutes.
A : How do I get there?
B : Walk straight until you come to the first traffic lights. Then, turn left and walk for five more minutes.

look for : 찾다
block : (미) 블록, (사방이 도로로 둘러싸인 도시의) 한 구획
I'd rather (= **would rather**) : ..... 하는 편이 더 좋다
traffic light : 신호등

Dialogue 4

A : Excuse me, I'm looking for a supermarket. Do you know where it is?
B : Are you looking for a big one or small one?
A : Well, I need to do some grocery shopping. Maybe a big one is better.
B : Um.... Lotte Mart is the biggest one in this neighborhood.
A : Is it far from here?
B : No, not really.
A : Which way should I go?
B : You cross the road over there, and go straight about 100 meters to the right. Then, you'll see the supermarket sign. You can't miss it.
A : Thank you, ma'am.

grocery : 식료잡화
neighborhood : 근처, 인근
You can't miss it : 곧(금방) 알 수 있어, 놓칠 수가 없어요

Dialogue 5

A : Excuse me, I think my friend and I are lost. I was wondering if you could help us.
B : What are you looking for?
A : We are trying to find the park that has the concert today.
B : Well, I'm not very familiar with this area because we moved here only a week ago. But I know there is a park down the road somewhere.
A : I see. .....
B : Do you know the name of the park?
A : Er..... It's Central Park.
B : I think it should be the one. You walk down the road, and if you can't find it, ask someone else there.
A : Thank you very much. I appreciate your help.
B : You're welcome. I hope you can find it soon.

lost : 길을 잃은
wonder : ..... 이 아닐까 생각하다, ... 인가 하고 생각하다
familiar : 익숙한, 잘 아는
area : 지역
move : 이사하다
down the road somewhere : 길 아래쪽 어딘가에 (있다)
someone (= somebody) else : 누군가 다른 사람

Useful Words and Expressions

1) Sentence Examples

Please tell me how I can get to your house?

Could you tell me where the library is?

Excuse me. Can you tell me the way to the hospital?

Is this the right way to the Hyatt Hotel?

How do I get to the drugstore?

Where is the nearest bank?

Is it a long way?

How far is it to the park from here?

Which direction should I take?

How long does it take to get there?

How can I get to the local market?

– I think, it's better to take bus number 13.

– Keep going straight, and you'll find the building on your right.

– Continue straight ahead for about 200 meters.

– Oh, you're going in the wrong direction.

– Just walk up / down the road.

– Turn left / right on 4th Avenue.

– No, it's quite near.

– It's just around the corner.

– Follow me. I'll show you the way.

– It's about a ten-minute walk.

– Sorry, I'm a stranger here myself.

2) Make sentences out of the words below.

1. You / find / the railway station / will / on the left.

_____

2. Now, / this street / go along / to the traffic lights.

_____

3. Can / tell me / the British Museum / you / where / is?

_____

3) Different Directions

Verbs

go straight ahead   **turn left**   **turn right**   **cross**   **go past**

- **Go straight ahead** for about 100 meters from exit 4.
- **Turn left** at the next traffic lights.
- **Turn right** when you see a roundabout.
- **Cross** the road and keep going for two blocks.
- **Go past** the old church and you will see the house.

Prepositions of Place

  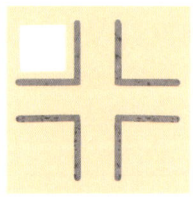  

next to   **opposite**   **at the corner of**   **between**   **in front of**

- The museum is **next to** Hyde Park.
- I live **opposite** the police station.
- It is located at **the corner of** Main Street and Fifth Avenue.
- The new KFC will **be between** Starbucks and McDonald's.
- Jane is standing **in front of** the bank.

Reading Comprehension - Japan

As a volcanically active country, Japan has thousands of onsens scattered throughout all of its major islands. Natural hot springs (溫泉, onsen) are numerous and highly popular across Japan. Unlike traditional public baths, onsens use naturally hot water from geothermally heated springs. At an onsen, all guests are expected to wash and rinse themselves thoroughly before entering the hot water. There are many types of hot springs, distinguished by the minerals dissolved in the water. Different minerals provide different health benefits, and all hot springs are supposed to have a relaxing effect on your body and mind. Hot spring baths come in many varieties, indoors and outdoors, gender separated and mixed, developed and undeveloped. Traditionally, onsens were located outdoors although a large number of inns have now built indoor bathing facilities as well. As most households have their own bath these days, the number of traditional public baths has decreased, but the number of sightseeing hot spring towns has increased.

volcanically : 화산으로, 화산 작용에의해
geothermally : 지열(地熱)로
distinguish : 구별하다, 분류하다
variety : 종류, 다양(성)
gender : 성, 성별(sex)

Conversation Practice

Please write your answers and practice with your partner.

Q1. Where is the nearest convenience store?

Q2. Can you give me directions to the nearest bus stop?
How do I get to the bus stop?

Q3. Please tell me how do I get to your house?
What's the best way to get to your house?

Q4. Where is the nearest supermarket?
What's the quickest way of getting to the supermarket?

Q5. Do you know where the train station is?
Can you tell me the best way to the train station from here?

Q6. I can't find a petrol station. Do you know where one is?

Q7. Have you ever lost your way? When and where?
What did you do then? Share your experience with others.

Unit 12 Appointment

"I want to make an appointment to see the doctor."

"Everything has beauty, but not everyone can see."
– Confucius –

Dialogue 1

A : Hi, James. What are you doing tonight? Do you have any plans?
B : No, nothing special. Why are you asking?
A : If you are free, maybe we can have some drinks together.
B : Well.... Actually, I'm quite tired. I'd rather not go out tonight.
A : Oh, that's a pity.
B : Anything urgent? How about tomorrow, then?
A : Tomorrow is fine. Where and what time shall we meet?
B : Shall we meet at 7 p.m. at the bar near my office?
A : Brilliant. I look forward to seeing you there.

    appointment vs. plan
     – appointment : 병원 진료예약이나 회의 등과 같은 공식적인 약속
     – plan : 친구와의 약속이나 여행 계획 같은 일상에서의 일반적인 약속
    That's a pity (= What a pity) : 그거 참 안됐군요. 유감이다
    urgent : 긴급한, 시급한
    brilliant : 훌륭한, 멋진 (보통 영국식으로 미국식의 great과 같은 의미)

Dialogue 2

A : Hello. Is it Dr. Kennedy's clinic?
B : Yes, it is. What can I do for you?
A : I want to make an appointment to see Dr. Kennedy.
B : Have you ever been here before?
A : No, it's my first time.
B : I see. When would you like to come?
A : How about this Thursday?
B : At what time?
A : Is it possible to see him at 9 a.m.?
B : No problem. May I have your name, please?
A : My name is Jane Woo.
B : Alright, Ms. Woo. Your appointment is made for this Thursday at 9 a.m. Please be here 10 minutes before the appointment time.
A : I will. See you on Thursday.

Dialogue 3

A : So, what are your plans for this weekend?
B : I don't know. Do you want to get together or something?
A : How about going to see a movie? I heard many good movies are showing now. Have you watched "Iron Man?"
B : No, I haven't. It's a good idea. Let's go to the movies this weekend.
A : Well, the movie is showing at 2 p.m., 4 p.m., 6 p.m., and 8 p.m. What time shall we go?
B : Why don't we go to the 4 p.m. showing? And we can go for dinner afterwards. I know there is a good Pizza House near the theatre.
A : That sounds like a good plan. Let's meet at the CGV movie theatre at 3:30 on Saturday.
B : Okay. See you on Saturday.

get together : 같이 어울린다, 모이다   get-together : 사교모임, 친목회
go to the movies : 영화보러 가다
afterwards (= afterward) : 후에, 나중에

Dialogue 4

A : Good afternoon, Sharon's Hair Salon. How may I help you?
B : Hi. I'd like to make an appointment to do my hair.
A : Sure. Who is your hair stylist?
B : Barry Tran.
A : When do you want to come?
B : Tuesday, 2 p.m. please.
A : I'm sorry, Barry is fully booked on that day. How about the next day?
B : Okay, then. Wednesday at the same time, 2 o'clock, please.
A : How about 2:30? Because he has another client at 2:00.
B : Well, that's fine with me.
A : Thanks for calling. See you on Wednesday.

do one's hair : 머리를 (어떤 스타일로) 하다, 머리를 손질하다
fully booked : 예약이 꽉 찬
client : 고객

Dialogue 5

A : Hello. I'd like to see Mr. Ford.
B : Do you have an appointment with him?
A : Yes, I do. I'm here for the job interview.
B : What's your name?
A : My name is Sarah Han.
B : Let me check for you, Ms. Han. ..... Your appointment is at 10:30. You are quite early, it's only 10 o'clock.
A : I know, I didn't want to be late for the appointment.
B : I'm afraid that Mr. Ford is in a meeting right now. Would you please wait at the lounge? You can have some coffee or tea while waiting. I'll let you know when he is ready.
A : Sure, no problem. Thank you.

Dialogue 6

A : Hello. Mr. Ford's office. This is Julia speaking.
B : Hi, this is Chris Thorn from YBC company. Can I speak to Mr. Ford?
A : I'm sorry. Mr. Ford is not in. May I take your message, Mr. Thorn?
B : Actually, I'm supposed to meet Mr. Ford tomorrow morning. But I have to cancel that appointment. There are some urgent matters came up in our head office, so I am flying out to London this afternoon.
A : I see. When will you return?
B : Well, I'm not so sure at the moment. Please tell him that I'll contact him by email to set our next business meeting.
A : All right. I'll do that.
B : I'm terribly sorry for the cancellation. And please send my apologies to him. This is something out of my control.

be supposed to + 동사원형 : .... 하기로 예정된 일을 언급할 때 사용한다.
  - You **are** not **supposed to** park the car here.
cancel : 취소하다
send my apologies : 나의 사과를 전하다
out of control : 통제할 수 없는, 제어가 불가능한
cancellation : 취소, 예약 취소
apology : 사과, 사죄

Useful Words and Expressions

1) Sentence Examples

Are you available this evening?

What time is our meeting today?

What are you doing tomorrow?

When is your appointment?

Have you made an appointment?

May I have an appointment with Dr. Kennedy on Monday?

Aren't we supposed to meet this afternoon?

Do you have any plans for this weekend?

Are you going to work on this coming Saturday?

What's your plan for the Christmas?

– Sorry. I already have some plans.

– Oh, the meeting has been canceled.

– We are going out on a picnic.

– At 11 o'clock on Thursday.

– No, I haven't.

– I'm sorry, he will be attending the seminar in Hong Kong on Monday.

– Yes, we are. But I'm afraid that I can't make it.

– Yes, we have a family gathering on Sunday.

– No. I don't usually work on weekends.

– I'm going to the Philippines.

2) Make sentences out of the words below.

1. Hi, James, / have / do / any plans / you / for tomorrow?

   _____

2. Have you made / to see / an appointment / Mr. Adams?

   _____

3. I'd like to / to see / Dr. Roberts / make an appointment / on Wednesday.

   _____

3) Prepositions of Time

Use different prepositions with different words.

at	in	on
at 10 o'clock at noon / midnight at lunch time at sunrise / sunset at the moment at Christmas	in the morning in March in winter in 2018 in six weeks / months in the future	on Friday morning on my birthday on weekends on time on December 25 on Christmas Day

4) Prepositions of Place

Use different prepositions with different words.

at	in	on
at the door at home at Jane's (house) at the supermarket at the airport at the top (of ....)	in bed in a car / taxi in Mexico in the hospital in the country in the sky	on a wall on a bus / plane on a balcony on the second floor on the way to work on Robinson Road

- Note : **home**은 "at"과 함께 쓸 수도 있고 생략할 수도 있다.
  be/stay at home or **be/stay home** (with or without "at")

Reading Comprehension - Vatican City

Vatican City is an independent city country located in Rome, Italy. It is the smallest country in the world, and its size is only one-sixth of Yeouido. Within the Vatican City are religious and cultural sites such as the Sistine Chapel. The chapel is the official residence of the Pope, and one of its functions is as a place for the election of new Pope. On the occasion of a conclave, a chimney is installed in the roof of the chapel, from which smoke arises as a signal. If white smoke appears, a new Pope has been elected, but if not, they will send up black smoke to signal that no successful result has yet happened. Even today, it is used for this purpose, including in the recent election of Pope Francis. The fame of the Sistine Chapel lies mainly in the frescoes that decorate the interior. It has some of the world's most famous paintings and sculptures, most particularly "The Last Judgment" and "The Creation of Adam." The ceiling, painted by Michelangelo, took four years to complete and is one of the most famous artworks of the Renaissance era.

chapel : 교회
conclave : 추기경들의 교황선거 회의
chimney : 굴뚝
paintings and sculptures : 그림들과 조각품들
fresco : 프레스코 벽화
artwork : 예술작품

Conversation Practice

Please write your answers and practice with your partner.

Q1. Are you free this evening?
　　Do you have time this evening?

Q2. Aren't we supposed to meet for lunch today?

Q3. Have you got any plans for tomorrow?
　　Do you have any plans for tomorrow?

Q4. May I have an appointment with Dr. Johns on Friday?

Q5. What time are we going to have the meeting this morning?
　　What time is our meeting this morning?

Q6. Would you like to make your next appointment now?

Q7. Shall we make a plan for the Christmas holidays?

Unit 13 Shopping

"I am looking for a birthday gift for my mother."

"If you are born poor it's not your mistake, but if you die poor it's your mistake."
– Bill Gates –

Dialogue 1

A : Hi, Jane. What are you doing?
B : Nothing much. I'm just relaxing at home. Why? What's going on?
A : You know, all the stores are having a summer sale now. So I was thinking, why don't we go shopping this afternoon? Would you like to go to the mall with me?
B : Um..... Actually, I don't need to buy anything.
A : Then, you can just browse and do window shopping. And perhaps, we can have some afternoon tea there.
B : Er..... all right, if you insist. I'll just keep you company.
A : Great. Thanks. You're such a wonderful friend.

browse : (가게 등에서) 상품을 쓱 훑어보다
window shopping : 사려는 의도 없이 진열된 상품을 들여다보고 다니는 것
keep (somebody) company : .... 와 동행하다, 함께 가다

Dialogue 2

A : Is there anything I can help you with, sir?
B : Well. I'm looking for a new laptop computer.
A : Do you have any particular brand in mind?
B : Not really. I used to have the LG notebook, but I lost it recently.
A : This one is very popular. It is light and has many new functions.
B : Looks good. How much is that?
A : It's 1,200 dollars.
B : It's nice, but too expensive for me. Do you have any special discounts or promotions?
A : Not today, but we'll have a bargain sale next week. We are going to have lots of special offers.
B : Good. I'll come back then.

particular brand : 특별한 브랜드, 특정 제품(상표)
function : 기능
promotion : 판촉, 판촉 상품

Dialogue 3

A : I'm looking for a birthday gift for my mother.
B : We have some perfumes, skin care products, and make-up items.
A : Hmm.... I'm not sure what to get. Any suggestion?
B : How old is she?
A : She is in her fifties.
B : How about a bottle of perfume? This Chanel No. 5 is quite popular for women in their fifties. Try it. ......
A : It smells nice.
B : Yes. This is very elegant smell, isn't it? And its fragrance lasts long, so you don't have to spray it many times. The bottle is so pretty. It'll be a perfect present for your mother.
A : Okay. I'll take this one. Could you please gift-wrap it for me?

women in their fifties : 50대 여성들
fragrance : 향기
gift-wrap : (리본 등으로 묶어) 선물용으로 포장하다

Dialogue 4

A : Excuse me. May I ask for your help?
B : Of course. How can I assist you?
A : I'm looking for the dress that is displayed at the window.
B : That's our new collection. What size do you wear? It comes in three sizes: Small, Medium, and Large.
A : I normally wear a size Medium.
B : We have it in black and light beige. Which one would you like to try?
A : I think I'd like to try a black one.
B : Here you go. You can try it on in the fitting room over there.
A : Thank you.
B : If you need any help, just let me know.

display : 진열하다, 전시하다
fitting room : 탈의실

Dialogue 5

A : Are you looking for something, ma'am?
B : Yes. I'm looking for a pair of sneakers for my son.
A : Do you want it for walking or running?
B : For running. My son plays sports all the time.
A : What about this one? This is the latest model from Nike. Most youngsters like this style.
B : Looks quite stylish. I'll take it.
A : We have two colors. Which color do you prefer, blue or gray?
B : I prefer the blue one.
A : Do you know his size?
B : Yes, he usually wears size 250.
A : Please, wait a moment. Let me see whether we have the size. ..... Sorry, I'm afraid we don't have that size in blue. How about the gray one? If your son doesn't like it, you can always bring it back.
B : Well, ... alright.
A : Thank you. Would you like to keep the box?
B : Yes, please.

a pair of sneakers : 운동화 한 켤레
- **a pair of** + **복수명사** : 두 개가 하나의 짝을 이루거나 두 부분이 붙어 하나로 된 사물을 가르키는 복수명사 앞에 쓰인다
- **a pair of** shoes/jeans/shorts/trousers/pajamas/glasses/scissors
- My **pajamas are** too big.
- I need **some** new **jeans** or I need **a** new **pair of** jeans.
- **Those are** nice **glasses** or That **is a** nice **pair of** glasses.

walking : 걷기, 산책, 보행
running : 달리기, 러닝
youngster : 젊은이
stylish : 멋진, 맵시 있는
wear : (옷, 모자, 장갑, 신발 등을) 입고 있다, 신고 있다
let me see / let's see : 그러니까, 어디 보자 (뭔가를 생각하거나 기억하려 할 때)
whether : .... 인지 어떤지
bring back : 반품하다, 다시 가져오다

Useful Words and Expressions

1) Sentence Examples

Where are we going?	- Let's go shopping.
Can I help you, sir?	- Yes. I'd like to see some cameras.
What's important to you?	- I want it to be small and light.
What brand is this?	- This is Canon.
Is it easy to use?	- Yes, it is very easy to use.
Are these on sale?	- No, not these ones.
Do you have any cheaper one?	- Let me show you something else.
How much does this television cost?	- It costs $2,500.
How much is the dress?	- It's ₩80,000.
Do you have any other color?	- We have it in blue.
What size is this?	- It's a medium.
Is someone looking after you?	- Yes, that sales lady is helping me.
What does your girlfriend like to do?	- She likes shopping.

2) Make sentences out of the words below.

1. There / at every store / a big sale / is / now.

   _____

2. What / usually / you / size / do / wear?

   _____

3. I / prefer / would / blue color.

   _____

4. Do / this camera / know / how much / you / is?

   _____

3) Practice the numbers

1	one
10	ten
100	one hundred
1,000	one thousand
10,000	ten thousand
100,000	one hundred thousand
1,000,000	one million
10,000,000	ten million
100,000,000	one hundred million
1,000,000,000	one billion

4) Practice the prices in won, dollars, and cents

₩500	five hundred won
₩1,000	one thousand won
₩25,000	twenty-five thousand won
₩300,000	three hundred thousand won
₩4,000,000	four million won
₩50,000,000	fifty million won
₩600,000,000	six hundred million won
$0.50	fifty cents
$1.00	one dollar
$2.00	two dollars
$7.50	seven dollars (and) fifty cents
$19.99	nineteen dollars (and) ninety-nine cents
$280.50	two hundred eighty dollars (and) fifty cents
$1,250.00	one thousand two hundred fifty dollars

5) English Vocabulary Words for Clothes, Shoes and Accessories

business suit	jacket / blazer	pants / trousers	shirt
tuxedo	polo shirt	jeans / denims	vest
dress	cardigan	skirt / miniskirt	T-shirt
evening gown	sweater	pajamas	swimsuit
coat / overcoat	blouse	shorts	tie / necktie
underwear	stockings	socks	leggings
hat	scarf	belt	(baseball) cap
(high-heel) shoes	boots	sneakers	sandals
handbag	clutch	wallet	(coin) purse

Reading Comprehension - Hong Kong

Hong Kong means "Fragrant Harbor" in Cantonese. The signature attraction of Hong Kong is the crowd of skyscrapers surrounding the waters of Victoria Harbour on Hong Kong Island; it is a really jaw dropping scene. There are more skyscrapers on this piece of land than anywhere else in the world. It's worth making time to see the skyline both in the day and at night. Most of all, it has the best city views in the world; the cityscape view remains one of the greatest man-made views on Earth. This can be viewed by the Peak walk, which takes you around the mountaintop admiring views of both the city and the South China Sea. The best way to get to the Peak is by the Peak Tram. The Peak Tram is, as most passengers agree, the only way to truly experience the beauty of the city's natural wonders. And tens of millions of people from every corner of the world have taken the ride, which offers a spectacular scenery of the city. Just watching the stunning cityscape of Hong Kong from the Peak would be a once in a lifetime experience to any visitors.

Cantonese : 광동어 (홍콩을 포함하여 중국 남서부에서 사용되는 중국어)
the crowd of skyscrapers : 많은 마천루 (초고층 빌딩)들
a jaw dropping scene : 입을 다물지 못할 정도의 광경
skyline : (산, 고층건물 등의) 하늘을 배경으로 한 윤곽
stunning cityscape : 놀랄만큼 멋진 도시풍경

Conversation Practice

Please write your answers and practice with your partner.

Q1. Which do you prefer, shopping online or going to a store?
Any why?

Q2. When do you usually go shopping?

Q3. What's your favorite store? And why?

Q4. What size do you normally wear?

Q5. Do you like shopping?
How much do you usually spend on clothes?

Q6. Have you ever asked for a discount on any item you bought?
And if so, what happened?

Q7. Have you ever bought any gift for your parents / friends?

Q8. Would you like that gift-wrapped?

Unit 14 Food

"What kind of food do you like?"

"The mind is everything. What you think you become."
– Buddha –

Dialogue 1

A : I'm starving. I didn't have time to eat my lunch. Shall we go for dinner now?
B : Where should we go?
A : That's a good question. Hmm.... How about Italian food?
B : Good idea. Do you know any good place?
A : Let's go to the new Italian restaurant near our office.
B : What sort of menu do they have?
A : They have Minestrone soup, Caprese salad, Margherita pizza, Lasagna, different kinds of pasta, ... and many more.
B : Sounds great. Have you tried there?
A : Once I tried Spaghetti Vongole there, and it was absolutely delicious.
B : Okay. Let's hurry. I'm getting hungry too.

I'm starving. : (구어) 배고파 죽겠다
absolutely : 완전히, 정말로

Dialogue 2

A : How do you like living in Korea, Tom?
B : It's great. People are nice, and I really like Korean food.
A : What's your favorite Korean food?
B : My favorite Korean food is Bulgogi.
A : It's a very popular dish to foreigners.
B : How about you? Do you like any American food?
A : My favorite American food is pizza.
B : That's yummy, but highly fattening. I prefer to eat more healthy food like vegetables and fruits.
A : I know, but I like all those junk foods like hamburger, pizza, coke, cakes, ... I think I should control myself, otherwise, I'll get fat.

fattening : 살찌는
junk foods : 허접한, 특히 칼로리가 많은 음식들

Dialogue 3

A : What time would you like to go out for lunch?
B : I think, I'll skip lunch today.
A : Why?
B : I'm on a diet because I'm fat now. I put on almost 5kg recently.
A : You don't look fat at all. You look just nice.
B : I don't think so. My clothes are all too tight. Every morning, I struggle to wear my clothes, and I hate looking at myself in the mirror.
A : If you don't eat lunch, you'll be hungry later on. Would you like me to get something for you? Something light?
B : Well, I'll just get some salad from the convenience store.

skip : 건너뛰다
be / go on a diet : 다이어트 하다
struggle : 애를 쓰다, 발버둥 치다
convenience store : 편의점

Dialogue 4

A : I'd like to have something sweet.
B : What do you have in mind?
A : Mmm..... How about icecream or chocolate?
B : Those are all too sweet. I don't like sweet things. How about some potato chips or corn chips instead?
A : They are crunchy but salty. I prefer something creamy and soft like icecream. Why don't we have some icecream for a change? You can choose something less sweet.
B : Do they have sherbet?
A : Yes, they have many flavors, strawberry, raspberry, mango, passion fruit, ...
B : Okay, then. I'll go for sherbet.

salty : 짭잘한, 소금기 있는
for a change : 기분 전환으로, 여느 때와 달리
go for (something) : .... 을 택하다

Dialogue 5

A : I think, I really need to start eating healthier.
B : I know what you mean. So I've changed my diet recently.
A : What kind of food do you usually eat?
B : I try my best to eat only fruits, vegetables, and chicken.
A : Is that really all you eat?
B : Yes. That's basically it.
A : How do you stick to only those foods?
B : Actually, fruits and veggies are really good for you.
A : I know, but what about the chicken?
B : I mainly eat baked chicken because it's a healthy way to eat it. There's not much fat, but a lot of protein.
A : That sounds delicious and nutritious.
B : You should try it. You won't be disappointed.

healthy - healthier - healthiest : healthy (건강한)의 비교급, 최상급
try one's best : 최선을 다하다
Is that all? : 그게 전부 입니까?
basically : 기본적으로, 근본적으로
stick to (something) : (바꾸지 않고) .... 을 고수하다, (어려움을 참고) .... 을 계속하다
veggies (= vegetables) : 야채
mainly : 주로, 대개는
baked chicken : 오븐에 구운 치킨
healthy way : 건강한 방식
fat : 지방
protein : 단백질
nutritious : 영양분이 많은
You should try it : 너도 한번 시도해 봐, 너도 한번 해봐
You won't be disappointed : 실망하지 않을거예요, 후회하지 않을거야

Useful Words and Expressions

1) Sentence Examples

What is your favorite cuisine?	– My favorite cuisine is Thai.
What's your favorite French dish?	– It's "Ratatouille."
Can you cook?	– Of course. I love cooking.
What time shall we have dinner?	– How about 7 o'clock?
Do you prefer fish or meat?	– I prefer fish.
Is your chicken alright?	– Okay, but it is pretty dry.
Do you like deep-fried food?	– Yes, I do. I love French fries.
How are your vegetables?	– The vegetables are kind of mushy.
Can I offer you some fruit?	– Yes, please.
What's your favourite fruit?	– I like peaches very much.
How often do you eat fresh fruit?	– Almost everyday.
Do you drink much coffee?	– No, I don't drink coffee at all.
May I have some tea?	– Sure. I'll make some tea for you.
What a wonderful dinner!	– I'm glad that you are enjoying it.
Are you on a diet?	– No, I'm not.
Uhh.... Pancakes? I ordered waffles.	– I'm so sorry, sir.

2) Make sentences out of the words below.

1. I / this dessert / love / because / are / the flavors / so good.

   _____

2. Do / for dinner / want to go out / you / this evening?

   _____

3. I / some cereal / have / just / in the morning / before I go to work.

   _____

3) English Vocabulary Words for Food

hot	tasty	bland	overcooked
warm	tasteless	salty	undercooked
lukewarm	hard	sweet	raw
cold	soft	sour	unripe
fresh	creamy	spicy	ripe
spoiled	chewy	bitter	oily
rotten	crunchy	tough	dry

4) Different Cooking Terms

bake	barbecue	boil / parboil	braise
fry / deep-fry	grill	simmer	microwave
sauté	steam	stew	roast

Reading Comprehension - Denmark

Nowadays, people are so afraid of being fat. In many societies, obesity often means ugly and unhealthy, and beauty and health are important elements of our life now. One thing comes to your mind when you think of Denmark is the "Danish Diet," commonly referred to as the "Royal Danish Hospital Diet," or the "Copenhagen Diet." It is a 13-day eating plan that promises massive weight loss, and recommends you to eat less carbohydrate but eat fat and protein as much as you like. Korea would not appear to be a country of large people, especially compared to urban centers in North America and Europe, but the situation is rapidly changing. The level of child obesity in Korea is broadly the same as the level in the US, mainly due to their western style diet. Not everyone, however, is convinced that obesity in Korea is that serious of a problem, especially compared to the issues of malnourishment and body image anxiety. So why not make permanent, sustainable lifestyle changes that include social support, keeping a food journal, and incorporating more physical activity into your daily routine.

obesity : 비만
carbohydrate : 탄수화물
malnourishment : 영양실조
sustainable : 지속할 수 있는, 유지할 수 있는
incorporate : 결합하다, 혼합하다

DANISH DIET

Conversation Practice

Please write your answers and practice with your partner.

Q1. What is your favorite food? Why do you like it so much?

Q2. How many meals do you usually have everyday?

Q3. Which do you prefer, Korean food or Chinese food?

Q4. What do you usually eat for lunch at school?
How much does your lunch usually cost?

Q5. Do you like pizza?
How often do you eat pizza?
What is your favorite pizza topping?

Q6. Do you like healthy food / junk food?

Q7. Do you always eat dinner with your family?

Q8. Do you like to try new food and drinks? If so, what are they?

Unit 15 Job

"What is the most interesting job in the world?"

"It's all about quality of life and finding a happy balance between work and friends and family."
− Philip Green −

Dialogue 1

A : You look serious. What are you thinking about?
B : I'm thinking about my future.
A : Really? After you graduate, what do you want to be?
B : Since I was young, I've always dreamed of becoming a flight attendant.
A : What do you like about the job?
B : Um.... I want to travel to many different countries around the world. And that job will give me the opportunity.
A : It would be interesting. But you may have to work irregularly and spend much time away from your home.
B : I understand it's not like ordinary office work. But I like to meet people from different cultural backgrounds, and I think, I can learn lots of new things by visiting different places.
A : You sound very positive and confident. Go for it. I wish you good luck with your future.

Dialogue 2

A : Hello, Jane. How are you getting along?
B : Well, I'm keeping myself busy.
A : Doing what?
B : I'm preparing for my job interview.
A : What kind of job are you applying for?
B : I'm applying for a flight attendant position at Korean Air.
A : That sounds great. When is the job interview?
B : It's coming soon, but I am not sure how well I can make it. I know that the competition is very high.
A : Don't worry. Just try your best. I'm sure you can do it well.
B : Thanks. I feel much better now. It was so nice to see you.

    keeping oneself busy : 자신을 바쁘게 하다
    apply for + job / position : .... 직업 / 직책에 지원하다
    apply to + company : ..... 회사에 지원하다
    competition : 경쟁
    I can make it : 내가 해낼 수 있다

Dialogue 3

A : Hi, Sarah. This is James. Haven't seen you for ages. How are you?
B : Hello, James. Long time, no see. How have you been?
A : Well, I've been busy for a while. Our company is expanding fast, and I am doing several projects at the same time.
B : No wonder. I haven't heard from you in a while.
A : I've been working all day and night. So I hardly see any friends these days.
B : Oh, that's not good. Don't work too hard. Otherwise, you'll be worn out.
A : I know. I guess I work too hard.
B : I think the most important thing in life is your health.
A : Thanks for your advice. Anyway, when you get a chance, let's meet up for a drink or something. So we can catch up.
B : Sure. Give me a call when you have time.

for ages : 오랫동안
expand : 확장하다
fast : 빠르게, 급속히
several projects : 몇 개의 프로젝트들
at the same time : 동시에
No wonder : ..... 하는 것이 당연하다, ... 은 조금도 이상하지 않다
in a while : 잠시동안, 한동안
hardly : 거의 .... 하지 않다
these days : 요즈음, 근래
otherwise : (만약) 그렇지 않으면
wear out : 지치게 하다
Thanks for your advice : 충고(조언) 해줘서 고마워
anyway : (문두에서) 그건 그렇고, 그런데
when you get a chance : 기회가 되면, 기회 있을 때
meet up : (특히, 약속을 하여) (....와) 만나다
Give me a call : 전화주세요

Dialogue 4

A : What do you do for a living, Sarah?
B : I am a teacher. I'm teaching at a primary school.
A : A teacher? That sounds like a lot of hard work.
B : Sometimes. But I like children. They are quite fun to be with.
A : Are there a lot of students in your class?
B : Most classes have about twenty-five to thirty students on average. And there are twenty-eight in my class.
A : Do you remember all their names?
B : Yes, I do. It's difficult at the beginning of the semester. But I try to memorize their names and call every student by their name.
A : So, do like your job?
B : Yes, it's quite rewarding. Teaching at primary school is easier than kindergarten. The students are less naughty.
A : I'm glad to hear that you enjoy your job.

hard work : 힘든 일, 고된 일
sometimes : 때때로, 가끔
a lot of (= lots of) : 많은
Most classes : 대부분의 클래스(학급)
on average : 평균적으로
memorize : 암기하다
in class : 수업 중에
rewarding : … 할 보람이 있는, … 할 가치가 있는
kindergarten : 유치원
naughty : 장난이 심한, 버릇없는
glad : 기쁜, 반가운

Dialogue 5

A : When are you going to work, Jane?
B : Tomorrow. I have a London flight tomorrow night.
A : What time does your duty start?
B : I have to be at the airport by 9:30 p.m.
A : Have you packed your bag?
B : I am packing now. Since it is winter, I'm bringing my thick winter coat, gloves, and my long boots.
A : How many days will you stay there?
B : We have a two-night stopover.
A : Do you have any plans this time?
B : I'm thinking to watch the musical "The Lion King."
A : What a brilliant idea. I heard it's spectacular. How many days off do you have after the flight?
B : I'll have three days off.
A : Let me know when you come back. So we can get together to celebrate your new job. I'll call Sarah and James to join us.
B : Thanks, Tom. That will be great.
A : Have a safe flight.

    duty : 직무
    pack : (짐 등을) 싸다
    thick winter coat : 두꺼운 겨울 코트
    gloves : 장갑
    boots : 부츠, 장화
    stopover : 단기 체류, 잠깐 들르는 곳
    watch : (시간과 관심을 기울이며) 보다, 지켜보다, 주시하다
    musical : 뮤지컬 (공연)
    spectacular : 장관의 구경거리의, 눈부신
    day off : 휴일
    celebrate : 축하하다

Useful Words and Expressions

1) Sentence Examples

Do you want to work?	– Of course. I need a job.
Are you working now?	– Yes, I'm doing part-time work.
What is your job?	– I'm a scientist.
What kind of job do you want?	– I want to be a flight attendant.
What company do you want to work for?	– I'm not sure yet. I have to think about it.
Where do you work?	– I'm working in Incheon.
Do you like your job?	– Yes, I do. / So so.
Can you manage your work well?	– I think I can.
Do you work hard?	– Yes, I work very hard.
Does your job have much stress?	– I get stressed out sometimes.
Did you work yesterday?	– Yes, I worked until 7 p.m.
Do you work on weekends?	– Sometimes, but not very often.
How long is your vacation?	– I have three weeks a / per year.

2) Make sentences out of the words below.

1. I / to work / very happy / am / with other people.

   _____

2. He / to complete his work / arrives early / always / on time.

   _____

3. She / a job / looking for / began / a long time ago.

   _____

4. Boss, / we / have a discussion / can / about my pay?

   _____

3) Different Jobs

flight attendant	teacher	accountant
secretary	soldier	architect
tour guide	nurse	athlete
receptionist	doctor	designer
pilot	businessman	driver
chef / cook	policeman	engineer
civil servant	salesman	lawyer
bank clerk	photographer	mechanic
office worker	reporter	programmer

Reading Comprehension - USA

Recently, the InSight spacecraft landed on Mars. InSight will study the deep interior of Mars, taking the planet's vital signs, its pulse and temperature. The National Aeronautics and Space Administration (NASA) of the United States explores and conducts scientific research on Earth systems, the solar system, and the universe. NASA research led to many of the goods and services we take for granted everyday. These include weather and communication satellites. A renowned physicist, Stephen Hawking predicted that humans wouldn't survive another 1,000 years on Earth alone without escaping beyond our fragile planet, while speaking at the Oxford Union debating society. "Remember to look up at the stars and not down at your feet. Try to make sense of what you see, wonder about what makes the universe exist. Be curious. However, difficult life may seem, there is always something you can do and succeed at. It matters that you don't just give up," he added.

spacecraft : 우주선
the planet's vital signs, its pulse : 행성의 생명에 관한 신호, 그것의 진동/파동
National Aeronautics and Space Administration (NASA) : 미국항공우주국
explore and conduct scientific research : 과학적 연구를 탐구하고 수행하다
take for granted : 당연한 일로 생각하다
fragile planet : 부서지기 쉬운 행성

Conversation Practice

Please write your answers and practice with your partner.

Q1. Are you looking for a job? / Do you want to work?

Q2. What kind of job would you like to have?
      Where do you want to work? And why?

Q3. Do you have a part-time job? If so, what do you do?
      How many days a week do you work?

Q4. What do you think would be the most interesting job / the least interesting job?
      And why?

Q5. Are you satisfied with your job? / Are you happy with your job?

Q6. Is your job stressful? / Do you get stressed with your job?

Q7. Are you an efficient worker?

PART 2

Passenger Address Announcement

Korea Air 144
Cathay Pacific Airways 150

Passenger Address Announcement

- Korean Air

Welcome

Good morning ladies and gentlemen.
One behalf of Captain Kim and the entire crew, welcome aboard Korean air, a member of Sky Team, flight _____ bound for _____.

Our flight time to _____ will be _____ hours and _____ minutes after take off. Please refrain from smoking at any time in the cabin and the lavatories. Also, the use of portable electronic devices is not allowed during take off and landing. If there is anything we can do to make your flight more comfortable, our cabin attendants are happy to serve you. Please enjoy your flight.
Thank you.

Safety Announcement

Ladies and Gentlemen,
The safety instruction card is in the seat pocket of the seat in front of you. Please read it. It shows you the equipment carried on this aircraft for your safety. A life jacket is in the seat pocket under your seat. To put it on, place it over your head, clip on the waistband and pull it tight. Please do not inflate it while you are still inside the aircraft. An evacuation slide and life raft is at each door. Your crew will direct you to your door. Additional emergency exits are shown on the leaflet.

In case of an emergency, oxygen masks will drop down in front of you. Please pull the mask down toward your face and place the mask over your mouth and nose. If you are traveling with a child, please attend to yourself first, then the child. Breathe normally, adjust the headband to suit yourself.

Departure

Ladies and gentlemen.
This is Korean Air flight _____ bound for _____. We are now just (a few/_____) minutes away from an on-time departure. Please make sure that your carry-on items are stowed in the overhead bins or under the seat in front of you. Also, please take your assigned seat and fasten your seat belt.
Thank you.

Seat Belt Sign Off

Ladies and gentlemen.
The captain has turned off the seatbelt sign, which means you can leave your seat if you wish. However, for your own safety and the safety of others around you, you must keep your seatbelt fastened while you are seated. Should the seatbelt signs come on again during the flight, please return immediately to your seat, and for everyone's safety, you must keep your belt fastened while seated.

Should you wish to remove anything from the overhead lockers, please take care as some items may have moved during take off and could fall out on you or other passengers.

Passengers are reminded that this is a non-smoking flight, which means that smoking is not allowed anywhere in the aircraft, including the toilets which are not protected by smoke detector alarms. As a reminder, the non-smoking sign will remain illuminated throughout the trip.

Service Procedure

Ladies and gentlemen.
We would like to briefly inform you about our service today.
we will begin our in-flight service starting beverages, and (breakfast / lunch/ dinner / a light meal) will follow. Also, in-flight sales will begin after the meal service is completed.

And approximately _____ hours _____ minutes prior to landing, (breakfast / lunch / dinner / a light meal) will be served. Thank you for choosing Korean Air. Have a pleasant flight.

Entertainment Service Announcement

(Magazine)
For your enjoyment during our flight today, we have placed a complimentary copy of our in-flight magazine, Morning Calm, in the seat pocket in front of you. If you wish, please feel free to take this with you when you leave.

(Sky-Shop)
Those interested in buying duty free goods will also find our Sky-Shop broucher in the seat pocket.

(Entertainment System)
If you are in the First or Business class sections, you will find controls for your reading light, call button and the in-flight entertainment system on the inside of your seat armrest. In the economy cabin, these controls are located on top of your seat armrest. To adjust your seat, push the round button beside the panel. Toilets for passengers seated in the economy cabins are located at the front, middle and rear of these cabins.

Tea, coffee and a full bar service will be available throughout the flight. If you require any special assistance, please contact a flight attendant nearest you. We are here to ensure that you have a comfortable and enjoyable flight. Later on we'll dim the cabin light, so you can get some rest. We recommended that while asleep, you keep your seatbelt fastened over the top of your blanket. This way, it will not be necessary to wake you up should the seatbelt signs come on during the flight. If you don't want to be waken for breakfast, please advise a flight attendant.
Thank you.

Arrival Information

(Korea)
Ladies and gentlemen.
All passengers entering into Korea are requested to have your entry documents ready. For your information, our flight number is KE _____ today's date is _____.

If you are carrying foreign currency more than 10,000 US dollars, or if you acquired more than 400 US dollars worth of articles abroad, please declare them on the customs form.

(USA)
Ladies and gentlemen.
In a moment, we will be distributing arrival cards and Customs and Quarantine declarations for U.S. There are three different US immigration forms and each passenger will be required to complete each forms, depending on your nationality, passport or visa status. There are no immigration requirements for US citizens.

If you hold a valid U.S. visa, you are required to complete a WHITE I-94 Immigration Form. If you are traveling under the U.S. Visa Waiver Programme, then you must complete a GREEN I-94 Immigration form. If you are not traveling under a U.S. visa, then you must fill out a BLUE I-94T immigration form.

We are required to ask you to fill out the forms in INK and in BIOCK letters, with alteration or cross outs. Please ask the flight attendant if you make a mistake and require another form. Each arriving traveler or head of family must complete the Customs Declaration form. This includes US citizens, Canadian citizens, Permanent residents of the United Stated and new immigrants to the USA. Passengers traveling beyond the U.S. are regarded as being in transit and are not required to fill out an arrival card.

(Australia)
The immigration card must be completed by, or on behalf of, all passengers including children. The immigration card must be completed accurately and in particular the question related to an address in Australia. In the event of an address being unknown this must be answered as "unknown." The Customs and Quarantine form must also be completed by all passengers. However, married couples traveling together with children under the age of 18 years only to complete one Customs and Quarantine form.
Thank you.

(New Zealand)

The immigration form must be completed by, or on behalf, all passengers including children. The Customs and Quarantine form must be completed by all passengers, except children 17 years or under who are traveling with a partner or legal guardian. Passengers under the age of 17 may be included on a parents' or guardians' declaration. Please note that the Immigration form and Customs and Quarantines are included in the Welcome to New Zealand book.
Thank you.

Turbulence

Ladies and gentlemen.
We will be passing through turbelence. Please return to your seat and fasten yur seat belt. Also, we will be suspending the beverage service. The service will be continued as soon as conditons improve.

Top of Descent Announcement

We hope you have enjoyed the in-flight entertainment. We are now preparing to land. The bar is closed and we will soon collect your headset. May I remind you to complete your arrival and immigration documentation by the time we arrive.

Headphone Collection

Ladies and gentlemen.
We hope you have enjoyed our in-flight entertainment. Our cabin attendant will be collecting your headphones.
Thank you.

Prepare for Landing

Ladies and Gentlemen.
Now we are approaching _____ international airport where the local time is _____.
At this stage, you should be in your seat with your seatbelt firmly fastened. Personal television screens, footrests and seat tables must be stowed away, and all hand luggage stored either in the overhead lockers or under the seat in front of you. Please ensure all electronic devices including laptop computers and computer games are turned off.

Farewell

Ladies and gentlemen.
We have landed at _____ international airport.
For your safety, please remain seated until the seat belt sign is turned off. When you open the overhead bins, be careful as the contents may fall out. And also, please have all your belongings with you when you deplane.
Thank you for flying Korean Air.

Passenger Address Announcement

– Cathay Pacific Airways

Welcome

Ladies and Gentlemen,
On behalf of Cathay Pacific and my team, welcome on board CX _____, our **one**world flight to _____ (destination)

To our Marco Polo Club members, it is a pleasure to see you again. For passengers interested in joining Asia Miles, application forms are available on board.

My name is _____ (first name), your Inflight Services Manager.
Captain _____ will take us to _____ (destination) in ____ hrs and _____ minutes.

We are looking forward to making your journey a pleasant and comfortable one. Please let us know if you need any assistance.

In preparation for take-off, please ensure your mobile phones and all electronic devices are switched off. All loose items including shoes, handbags and laptop computers must be stowed under the seat in front of you or in the overhead compartments.

Thank you and enjoy the flight.

Safety Demonstration Announcement

Ladies and Gentlemen, welcome aboard this Cathay Pacific Aircraft. As Safety is our priority, please take a few moments to review the following presentation.

Mobile phones must be switched off until the aircraft lands and cabin doors are open. Transmitting devices such as Walkie-talkies and remote control devices must not be used on the aircraft. All other electronic devices should also be switched of until 15 minutes after take-off, as these can interfere with aircraft instruments and systems.

For take-off and landing, hand baggage and loose items must be placed under the seat in front of you, or stowed in the compartments provided. Please be careful to ensure items placed in the overhead compartment do not fall out when the compartment is opened. The aisles and exits must be kept clear of baggage and any obstructions.

Seat belts are fastened and adjusted as shown. To unfasten the seat belt, lift the buckle. For Business Class, seat belts are fastened and adjusted as shown. To unfasten the seat belt, press the red release button. Children under 2 years old must use a "Child restraint device" when the seat belt sign is on.

We strongly recommend that you keep your seat belt fastened as there may be unexpected turbulence during the flight. If Oxygen is required, masks will drop automatically. Pull the mask down, place it over your nose and mouth. Adjust the strap. Breath normally. Attend to yourself before helping children or others. A life Jacket is stowed under the seat or in the armrest. Place the life jacket over your head. Secure the tape firmly around your waist. Inflate your life jacket when leaving the aircraft by pulling the red toggle firmly down, or by blowing into the tube. To attract attention, there is a whistle and a light. Infant life jackets and Flotation Cots are also carried on board.

In an emergency, or when you hear "Brace, Brace" - adopt the brace position which is shown in the safety instruction card. Escape path lighting is located along the aisles. The light will be ON in an emergency. Exits are equipped with slides to assist an evacuation. Our Cabin Crew are pointing out your nearest exit now.

This is a non-smoking flight. There are smoke detectors with alarms in every toilet. Smoking in the cabin and toile is forbidden under Hong Kong Law. Offenders are liable to a fine and imprisonment.

We will soon be taking-off. Please ensure that your hand baggage, tables and televisions are safely stowed, seatbacks are in the take off position and your seat belt is fastened.

Please read the safety card in the seat pocket. If you have any questions, please ask a member of our Cabin Crew.

After Take-Off

Ladies and Gentlemen,
We will shortly be serving drinks and _____. Snacks and drinks will be available throughout the flight. Before arrival in _____, we will be serving _____.

- Inflight Entertainment / Health Video / Change For Good Announcement

For your entertainment, we have a wide selection of video and audio channels. Program details can be found in the Studio^{cx} section of the Discovery magazine. Our inflight entertainment will be available soon.

To help you feel more comfortable and relaxed during your flight, 'Healthy Flying' tips can be found in the Discovery Magazine.

We will shortly handing out Change for Good envelopes. Please support UNICEF by donating any spare change into the envelopes. Your contributions are highly appreciated.

Turbulence

Ladies and Gentlemen, we are passing through an area of turbulence, please fasten your seat belts. Thank you.

(If applicable) (e.g. during meal service)
We regret to advise you that we are unable to serve hot drinks at this time.

Descent

Ladies and Gentlemen,
We are now descending into _____ (airport). The local time is _____, and the ground temperature is _____ degrees Celsius, or _____ degrees Fahrenheit.

Would you kindly return to your seats and stow all your belongs, including loose items, shoes and handbags. Place your seat back upright, stow your table and footrest, and check that your seatbelt is securely fastened.

Electronic devices such as laptop computers must be turned off and stowed under the seat in front of you or in the overhead compartments. Mobile phones must be switched off until the "Seat Belt" sign has been turned off.

In a few minutes, we will be collecting your headsets and UNICEF donations.

Transit PA

- Transit Passengers Must Remain On Board

Ladies and Gentlemen,
It is security requirement that all transit passengers remain onboard. During our stopover, please collect all your belongings, as a security check will be conducted. Please return to your original seats and avoid using the toilets, so that we can clean and prepare the cabin. Thank you for your cooperation. Our stopover time will be as brief as possible.

– Transit Passengers Must Disembark

Ladies and Gentlemen,
For security reasons, all passengers are requested to leave the aircraft and proceed to the transit lounge. Please take all your belongings with you as any items left behind will be

removed. Please return to your original assigned seat when reboarding the aircraft.

Thank you for your cooperation. Our stopover time will be as brief as possible.

After Landing

Ladies and Gentlemen,
Welcome to _____ (City)

It is a safety requirement that you remain seated with your seatbelt fastened until the aircraft has stopped and the seatbelt sign has been turned off.

Please be careful when opening the overhead compartment, as items inside may fall out. Please ensure that you have all your belongings before leaving the aircraft. Our ground staff will be available to help you on arrival.

It has been a pleasure looking after you and we hope to see you again. Thank you for flying Cathay Pacific, a member of the **one**world alliance.

PART 3

Appendix

Useful Phrasal Verbs   158
Irregular Verbs   164

Useful Phrasal Verbs

along	**bring along** : …을 갖고가다, 데려가다 - Can I **bring** a friend **along** to the party? **get along** : 잘 지내다 - He doesn't **get along** well with his father. **go along** : 나아가다, 계속하다 - I'll explain the rules as we **go along**.
around	**bring around** : (사람, 물건을) 데리고 오다 - We gradually **brought** her **around** to our point of view. **look around** : 둘러보다 - Have you had a chance to **look around** the house? **show** (somebody) **around** : 안내하다, 구경시켜 주다 - The real estate agent **showed** us **around** the house.
at	**aim / point** (something) **at** : 겨냥하다, 겨누다 - **Aim** the gun **at** the target. **guess at** : 짐작하다 - I can't even **guess at** what you mean. **hint at** : … 을 암시하다 - The facts **hinted at** a solution to the problem. **laugh at** : … 을 보고 웃다, … 을 비웃다 - I look so silly. People will **laugh at** me. **look at** : 바라보다 - **Look at** the sky. Isn't it so beautiful? **shout at** (somebody) : …에게 고함치다 - Dad really **shouted at** me when I broke the window. **stare at** : … 을 응시하다 - The boxers **stare at** each other's eyes. **throw** (something) **at** (somebody) : … 을 … 에게 던지다 - They **threw** eggs **at** the mayor.
away	**put** (something) **away** : 치우다, 정리 정돈하다 - The children **put** their toys **away**. **take away** : 가져가다 - They're going to **take** my citizenship **away**. **throw away** : 버리다 - Don't **throw away** these books. I need them.

back	**bring back** : 돌려주다, 가지고 돌아오다 - He **brought back** his library books. **give back** : 되돌려주다, 반환하다 - You can borrow my CD, as long as you promise to **give** it **back**. **hold back** : 제지하다, 자제하다 - He is so enthusiastic. It's hard to **hold** him **back**. **pay** (somebody) **back** : 빌린 돈을 갚다 - I'll **pay** you **back** as soon as possible. **set back** : 퇴보시키다, 저지하다 - This could **set back** the project by several months.
down	**break down** : (차, 기계 등이) 고장나다 - He was late for the meeting because his car **broke down**. **chop down** : (나무 등을) 베다 - Why did you **chop down** the tree in your yard? **cut down** (**on** something) : (먹거나, 마시는 것을) 줄이다 - I'm trying to **cut down on** coffee. I drink too much of it. **let down** : 실망시키다 - I will not **let** you **down**. **play down** : 경시하다 - He **played down** the importance of the news. **pull down** : (건축물을) 헐다 - Many old buildings are **pulled down**.
down	**slow down** : 속도를 줄이다 - You are driving too fast. **Slow down**. **tear down** : (건물을) 부수다 - They are going to **tear down** the church. **track down** : (추적하여) 찾아내다 - The police finally **tracked** him **down** at the theatre.
in	**believe in** : …. 을 믿다 - Do you **believe in** God? **call in** : 불러들이다, (도움을) 청하다 - I think it's time we **call in** an expert.

in	**fill in (= fill out)** 작성하다, 기입하다 - Please **fill in** this immigration form. **get in** : (차에) 타다 - Henry **got in** the car and drove away. **hand in** : 제출하다 - The students **handed** their assignments **in** to the teacher. **phase in** : 단계적으로 끌어들이다 - The new program will be **phased in** gradually. **take in** : 흡수하다, 섭취하다 - We tried to **take in** the new information. **trade in** : (물품을) 대가의 일부로 제공하다 - Why don't you **trade in** your old refrigerator for a new one.
off	**call off** : 취소하다 - We **called off** the meeting. **get off** : (버스, 기차, 비행기에서) 내리다 - He **got off** the train at Paddington Station. **go off** : (폭탄이) 폭발하다, (경보, 시계, 알람 등이) 울리다 - A bomb **went off** at the airport. **lay off** : 해고하다 - The company **laid off** fifty workers.
off	**put off** : 연기하다, 기다리게 하다 - The council **put off** the meeting for a week. **see** (somebody) **off** : …. 를 배웅하다 - A large crowd gathered at the airport to **see** him **off**. **take off** : (비행기가) 이륙하다 - The airplane **took off** on time. **turn off** : (라디오, TV, 수도, 가스 등을) 잠그다, 끄다 - He **turned off** the radio.
on	**depend on** : …. 에 의지하다, …. 에 의존하다 - I don't want to **depend on** anyone. **get on** : (버스, 기차, 비행기에) 타다 - Alison **got on** the bus outside the school.

on	**go on** : 계속하다, 지속되다 - How long will this hot weather **go on**? **hold on (= hang on)** : 기다리다 - Please **hold on** a minute, I'll be right back. **keep on** : 계속하다 - Are you going to **keep on** singing all night? **move on** : 계속 앞으로 나아가다 - Let's **move on** to the next subject. **put on** : 입다 - Can I **put** it **on**? **take on** : (일, 책임 등을) 떠맡다 - When John was sick, a friend **took on** his work at the office. **try on** : 입어보다 - Is it possible to **try** it **on**? **turn on** : (전등, TV, 라디오 등을) 켜다 - Can you **turn on** the TV?
out	**carry out** : 실행하다, 수행하다 - An investigation is being **carried out** by the police.
out	**cut out** : 잘라내다 - I **cut out** a beautiful picture in the magazine. **drop out** : (학교, 대학, 경기 등을) 그만두다, 뒤떨어지다 - Edward went to college but **dropped out** later. **hand / give** (something) **out** : .... 을 나누어 주다 - One of your jobs is to **hand out** the prizes. **try out** : ....을 테스트해 보다 - Would you like to **try out** our products, too? **walk out** : 나가버리다, (항의하고) 퇴장하다 - She just **walked out** of the room. **work out** : 운동하다 - He **works out** at the gym everyday.
over	**get over** : (장애, 혼란 등을) 극복하다 - I'm trying to **get over** my fear of flying.

over	**hand over** : 넘겨주다, 양도하다 – We have to **hand** the evidence **over** to the police. **knock over** : (컵, 사람 등을) 엎지르다, 넘어뜨리다 – I am sorry. I didn't mean to **knock** you **over.** **pull over** : (차를) 길가에 붙이다 – Can you just **pull over** here, so I can get out. **take over** : 떠맡다, 인계받다 – They will **take over** at the beginning of September. **talk over** : …. 에 관해 의논하다 – Let's **talk** it **over** before we decide.
up	**break up** : (남녀의 사이를) 갈라놓다, (결혼, 우정을) 끝내다 – Why did you **break up** with your boyfriend? **bring** (something) **up** : (화제를) 꺼내다 – Please don't bring it up again. **catch up** (**with** somebody) : (사람, 차, 나라 등을) 따라잡다 – I'm not ready yet. You go on and I'll **catch up with** you.
up	**cheer up** : 격려하다, 기운을 내다 – She tried to **cheer up** the players. **clean up** : 청소하다, 정리하다 – Alice took two hours to **clean up** the house. **end up** (somewhere) : 마침내 (…. 으로) 되다 – You could **end up** in the hospital due to flu complications. **fill up** : 가득 채우다 – I **filled up** the glass with water. **give up** : 포기하다 – Just don't **give up** even though it's difficult. **grow up** : 자라다, 어른이 되다 – Children **grow up** with so many problems in today's world. **hang up** : (전화를) 끊다 – After receiving a busy signal, I **hung up** the phone. **hurry up** : 서두르다 – Please **hurry up**. You don't have much time. **keep up** (**with** somebody) : (사람, 흐름 등에) 뒤떨어지지 않다 – You're running too fast. I can't **keep up with** you.

up	**look up** : 올려다보다, 쳐다보다 – She **looked up** from her book as I entered the room. **make up** : 만들어 내다, 메우다 – She likes to **make up** stories. **mix up** : 혼동하다, 착각하다 – I think most people **mix up** race and culture. **pick up** : 가져오다, 집어들다, (지식 등을) 익히다 – You may **pick up** the documents at the office. **speak up** : 크게 말하다 – I can't hear you. Could you **speak up** a little, please? **sum up** : 요약하다 – He **summed up** the discussion in two minutes. **tear up** : 찢다, 잡아 벗기다, 파기하다 – Don't you dare **tear up** her ticket. **wake up** : 잠에서 깨다 – My grandmother often **wakes up** in the middle of the night.

Irregular Verbs

현재	과거	과거분사	현재	과거	과거분사
be	was/were	been	hit	hit	hit
beat	beat	beaten	hold	held	held
become	became	become	hurt	hurt	hurt
begin	began	begun	keep	kept	kept
bite	bit	bitten	know	knew	known
blow	blew	blown	leave	left	left
break	broke	broken	lend	lent	lent
bring	brought	brought	let	let	let
build	built	built	lie	lay	lain
buy	bought	bought	light	lit	lit
catch	caught	caught	lose	lost	lost
choose	chose	chosen	make	made	made
come	came	come	mean	meant	meant
cost	cost	cost	meet	met	met
cut	cut	cut	pay	paid	paid
do	did	done	put	put	put
draw	drew	drawn	quit	quit	quit
drink	drank	drunk	read	read	read
drive	drove	driven	ride	rode	ridden
eat	ate	eaten	ring	rang	rung
fall	fell	fallen	rise	rose	risen
feel	felt	felt	run	ran	run
fight	fought	fought	say	said	said
find	found	found	see	saw	seen
fly	flew	flown	sell	sold	sold
forget	forgot	forgotten	send	sent	sent
get	got	gotten	shine	shone	shone
give	gave	given	shoot	shot	shot
go	went	gone	show	showed	shown
grow	grew	grown	shut	shut	shut
hang	hung	hung	sing	sang	sung
have	had	had	sit	sat	sat
hear	heard	heard	sleep	slept	slept
hide	hid	hidden	speak	spoke	spoken

현재	과거	과거분사
spend	spent	spent
stand	stood	stood
steal	stole	stolen
swim	swam	swum
take	took	taken
teach	taught	taught
tear	tore	torn
tell	told	told

현재	과거	과거분사
think	thought	thought
throw	threw	thrown
understand	understood	understood
wake	woke	woken
wear	wore	worn
weep	wept	wept
win	won	won
write	wrote	written

Answer Key

Make sentence out of the words below

Unit 1 Greetings

1. How are you getting along?
2. Oh, I haven't seen you for ages.
3. It was my pleasure to meet you.
4. Tom, may I introduce my friend, Oliver Thorn?

Unit 2 Family

1. There are five people in my family.
2. How many cousins do you have?
3. My father teaches at school and my mother is a housewife.

Unit 3 Hobby

1. What kind of movie do you like?
2. I like outdoor sports very much.
3. He went swimming before breakfast this morning.
4. Do you go for a run every morning?

Unit 4 School

1. Have you finished your homework?
2. Richard wants to go to college to study economics.
3. Do you remember what time our class starts tomorrow?

Unit 5 Travel

1. I want to go on a tour to Japan in November.
2. Oliver is going on a trip to Turkey next month.
3. How long does it take to cross the Atlantic by ship?
4. Could you please leave your contact number?

Unit 6 Airport

1. Would you mind opening your briefcase?
2. We are going to Toronto to visit some friends of ours.
3. Your luggage will be transferred to your next flight automatically.
4. Which seat would you prefer, a window seat or an aisle seat?

Unit 7 Airplane

1. How long does it take to get from Hong Kong to Sydney?
2. It takes about 11 hours from Seoul to Amsterdam.
3. Are there any vacant seats at the back of the plane?

Unit 8 Hotel

1. The hotel we stayed at was near the beach.
2. I'd like some information about hotels in New York.
3. The room was comfortable and everyone was very friendly.
4. May I put your luggage on the table, sir?

Unit 9 Restaurant

1. Are you ready to order ma'am?
2. We'd like to offer you our apologies for the trouble.
3. How would you like your steak, sir?

Unit 10 Weather

1. Do you know what the weather is going to be like next week?
2. It has been raining since this morning and it's still raining.
3. The temperature in Seoul was 33 degrees yesterday.

Unit 11 Directions

1. You will find the railway station on the left.
2. Now, go along this street to the traffic lights.
3. Can you tell me where the British Museum is?

Unit 12 Appointment

1. Hi, James, do you have any plans for tomorrow?
2. Have you made an appointment to see Mr. Adams?
3. I'd like to make an appointment to see Dr. Roberts on Wednesday.

Unit 13 Shopping

1. There is a big sale at every store now.
2. What size do you usually wear?
3. I would prefer blue color.
4. Do you know how much this camera is?

Unit 14 Food

1. I love this dessert because the flavors are so good.
2. Do you want to go out for dinner this evening?
3. I just have some cereal in the morning before I go to work.

Unit 15 Job

1. I am very happy to work with other people.
2. He always arrives early to complete his work on time.
3. She began looking for a job a long time ago.
4. Boss, can we have a discussion about my pay?

Note

Note

References

Korean Air In-flight Announcement Manual
Cathay Pacific Airways Passenger Address Announcement Handbook
Cathay Pacific Airways Inflight Service Manual
Basic Grammar in Use, CAMBRIDGE UNIVERSITY PRESS
Grammar in Use Intermediate, CAMBRIDGE UNIVERSITY PRESS
Practical English Usage, Oxford University Press and YBM
English Communication 1, DARAKWON
English Communication 2, DARAKWON

저자소개

김애경

숭실대학교 경영학 석사
숭실대학교 경영학 박사수료
전) 배재대학교 항공운항과 외래교수
　　Cathay Pacific Airways 수석사무장
현) 원광보건대학교 항공서비스과 겸임교수

http://blog.naver.com/learners_world

박인주

공주대학교 경영학 석사
공주대학교 경영학 박사
전) 대한항공 객실승무원
　　Cathay Pacific Airways 객실승무원
현) 원광보건대학교 항공서비스과 부교수

**Practical English
for
Airlines and Tourism**

펴 낸 날   2019년 3월 4일

지 은 이   김애경, 박인주
펴 낸 이   최지숙
편집주간   이기성
편집팀장   이윤숙
기획편집   정은지 최유윤 이민선
표지디자인   정은지
책임마케팅   임용섭, 강보현
펴 낸 곳   도서출판 생각나눔
출판등록   제 2008-000008호
주   소   서울시 마포구 동교로 18길 41, 한경빌딩 2층
전   화   02-325-5100
팩   스   02-325-5101
홈페이지   www.생각나눔.kr
이 메 일   bookmain@think-book.com

- 책값은 표지 뒷면에 표기되어 있습니다.
  ISBN 978-89-6489-961-8   13740

- 이 도서의 국립중앙도서관 출판 시 도서목록(CIP)은 서지정보유통지원시스템 홈페이지 (http://seoji.nl.go.kr)와 국가자료공동목록시스템(http://www.nl.go.kr/kolisnet)에서 이용하실 수 있습니다(CIP제어번호: CIP2019006971).

Copyright ⓒ 2019 by 김애경 박인주, All rights reserved.
- 이 책은 저작권법에 따라 보호받는 저작물이므로 무단전재와 복제를 금지합니다.
- 잘못된 책은 구입하신 곳에서 바꾸어 드립니다.